For David & Robin,

RECIPES FROM
221
South Oak Bistro
TELLURIDE, CO

by

Eliza H.S. Gavin

Telluride - Come for the snow.
Stay for the food!

ISBN #978-0-578-01054-0

For more information write to:
Goodall L.L.C.
PO Box 1158
Telluride, Colorado 81435

Photography by
Ben Edmonson and Doug Berry

Design and Production by
Tor Anderson / True North Designworks

Dedication

I dedicate this book book to my beautiful son, Gigger. Also to my brother, Rob, and his blossoming family. And of course to Gavin, my wonderful husband.

TABLE OF CONTENTS

Starters

Soups

Salads

Main Courses

Desserts

Index

Acknowledgments

Thanks to the present and past team at 221, without whom there would be no 221. A special thanks to Brent Englund, Bill Thomas, Gail Serviss, Dave Sinclair, Simon Collins, Shane LeBlanc, Paul Riley, Bear Guenther and Chad Glidewell. A big thanks for all of my guinea pigs, especially Gavin, Rob and Sara Goodall and their friends, the Currys, the Johnsons, the crew from the Big Island and anyone else who's attended one of my experimental cocktail and recipe testing parties. Thanks to Buzz and Susan Goodall for their continued support. Also thanks to Tor Anderson with his design and production work and Ben and Doug for snapping the beautiful photos. A big shout out to 221's dishwashers, Oscar, Raul, Rene, Jose, Angel and CJ. You do more than you know.

Introduction

221 SOUTH OAK BISTRO HAS CONSUMED my life for almost ten years. From taking reservations and talking to the guests to developing recipes and prepping, as a chef/owner my responsibilities vary from day to day. My favorite job is running our hectic kitchen line. On the line, one must move quickly at the behest of the servers and their tickets. Reaction time is everything, as the food must be beautifully presented and piping hot. I love moving at such a fast pace.

The kitchen line at 221 is small and narrow. On the end is the dishwasher, who must bob and weave among all of the bodies to deliver and retrieve the dirty items. Then comes the hot station or the "everything" station. This team member must run the fryer, provide vegetables and cook the meats to perfection. Next is the salad station. Along with salads, this team member must help the hot station whenever possible by running the fryer and setting up sides. The end of the line is the expo station, which is where I usually am. The expo cooks all fish, soups, most of the appetizers and plates all of the hot food. All of these stations can be a juggle but they're fast and fun.

I love working the line. All of the stress and pressure to get the food out hot and cooked just right is a thrill. At the end of a tough night, I feel tired and sweaty but completely content. When servers call out "Compliments to the Chef," I have a great feeling of accomplishment.

With my first pregnancy, I had to give up the line. Gavin and I decided the heat and stress was too much for baby Gigger. I was quite cranky, having to stay in the well-ventilated basement and prep. It did not hold nearly the same excitement, working at my own pace and not at the speed of the tickets. I knew it was the right thing to do. Thus, I eventually gave in and stood at the end of the line to help out a bit and make sure everything was running smoothly. Come summer, I'll work the line again, but until then, I'll be keeping busy with the other hundred tasks that need to be done.

221 transforms my nervous energy into productivity. I hear it calling me, in the morning and late at night. Its many responsibilities keep me awake. The happiness of the guests and my staff races through my mind during workouts. Will that shelf hold until I can get that two by four?

I remember the first time I ate at 221. It was in October of 1999. My dining partner and I sat at table eleven and enjoyed an abbreviated off season menu. I had a special feeling about the space. That December, I dropped my resume around town and had some pretty good offers. I held out for a mediocre offer from 221. I knew that's where I belonged. After a year, I approached the owners and made them an offer. On my twenty-seventh birthday, I opened my first restaurant.

The business came with quite a bit of necessary equipment, tables, chairs, stoves, fridges and most importantly, Brent. This dynamic front of the house manager, is an integral piece of 221 and I appreciate his knowledge of wine, team building, client relations and Red Sox stats.

The structure that stands at 221 South Oak street was built in the 1890's and was originally three small shacks. Former tenants, relate stories of frozen pipes, thin walls and ghosts. I have yet to see a ghost but know some who have. It was refurbished in 1993 and is the restaurant you see today.

I am the third Chef and the third owner of 221 South Oak Bistro. It has taught me heaps. This little house has provided me with a creative output and has matured me in a number of ways. As with running any business, you must be flexible and dependable. When something as unstable as food is involved, the level of difficulty increases. I've accidentally bought cases of meats or vegetables and have had to develop new ways of serving them.

Creativity with cooking must be quick because food is in a constant state of flux. It is the instability of food that makes the craft of cooking so challenging. I refer to cooking as a craft rather than an art because of its usefulness.

I hope you find these recipes useful. It was a fun challenge to assemble this book. I thought it would be easy, especially since I've been cooking these recipes for years. I found, once again, that anything worth doing is not easy. Some of the dishes are a bit difficult for the home cook but all are fun and delicious. ■

Starters

I believe the beginning of a meal sets the stage for the performance and a starter should blow the guest away in the first act. I like to pack my appetizers full of complex flavors. It can be difficult developing a dish that will wow a guest but also be produced in a short time. Most of these recipes use different stations in the kitchen to produce a single dish. This allows different elements and methods to be showcased on one plate.

Menage á Foie: Praline Crusted Foie Gras, Pâté de Foie Gras & Grilled Foie Gras with Ham

Serves 8

Skyler visits us annually and he always orders the Foie Gras. On one of his first visits, he suggested that I change the name from Foie Gras Three Ways to Menage á Foie. Clever indeed. Thank you Skyler.

The silky texture of Foie Gras is achieved by overfeeding ducks until their livers account for one-quarter of their body weight. I've been told the ducks enjoy the process and line up to be fed.

This recipe does require some juggling between the seared and grilled foie gras. You may cook one of the preparations and then the other but do not plate the former preparation. The fat from the foie gras will ooze out onto the plate and make a mess. It's best to plate when both of the preparations are ready and your guests are sat.

Spicy Cherry Relish

2 dried chili d'arbols

1 1-inch knob of ginger, peeled

1 6-ounce can of pineapple juice

¼ cup red wine vinegar

2 cups fresh cherries, pitted and chopped

1 cucumber, peeled, seeded and small diced

1 lobe grade-A Foie Gras

Pâté de Foie Gras

1 tablespoon Olive Oil

½ cup duck or chicken liver (not foie gras), cleaned

2 shallots, chopped

½ cup Port Wine

3 tablespoons unsalted butter, softened

8 toast points

Praline Crusted Foie Gras

¼ cup pecans

¼ cup brown sugar

Grilled Foie Gras

½ pound Virginia Ham, thinly sliced

1 **Spicy Cherry Relish**: In a blender, combine the chilis, ginger, pineapple juice, red wine vinegar and ¼ cup of the cherries. Blend until smooth. Pour this mixture over the cucumbers and remaining cherries. Stir to combine. Chill the relish overnight. It will keep, refrigerated for 2 weeks and gets better as it ages.

2 **Allow the Foie Gras to sit** at room temperature until it is malleable. Once it is soft, separate the lobes and remove any stringy veins. Slice the lobes into 1 ½-ounce portions and chill. Reserve any scraps for the pâté.

3 **Pâté de Foie Gras**: Get a cast iron pan very hot. Add the olive oil to the pan and heat until it shimmers. Salt the duck liver and add half to the hot pan and cook for 30 seconds. Add the foie gras scraps as well as the shallots and sear on all sides, for about 30 seconds. Add the port and bring the mixture to a boil. Reduce the port by half. Pour the hot mixture over the remaining livers and chill the mixture for 1 hour.

4 **Place the liver mixture in a food processor.** Run the machine and add the softened butter. Continue to run the machine until the pâté is smooth. Chill the pâté until it is firm, at least 6 hours.

5 **Praline Crusted Foie Gras & Grilled Foie Gras**: Light the grill. In a food processor, place the pecans and brown sugar. Chop the nuts and sugar until they form a coarse meal. Heat a cast iron pan over a high heat. Generously Salt 8 portions of foie gras. When the pan smokes, add the foie gras. Reduce the heat to medium and allow the foie gras to sear. When a brown crust has formed on the down side, flip the foie gras. Sprinkle the foie gras with the pecan mixture and cook until it is just soft in the middle, about 3 minutes. Keep the foie gras warm. Place the other portions of foie gras on the grill. Do not place them on the center of the grill as this makes it harder to remove. Rather place them on the cooler edges. Allow the foie gras to cook for 2-3 minutes. Quarter turn the grilled foie gras, thus making nice marks and allow to cook for 2 minutes. Flip the foie gras and grill until just cooked through, about 2-4 minutes depending on the heat of your grill . Grill the slices of ham until warm.

6 **Place a spoonful of Pâté de Foie Gras** on a toast point. On a plate, place the Pâté de Foie Gras, the Praline Crusted Foie Gras and the Grilled Ham with the Grilled Foie Gras atop. Serve with the Spicy Cherry Relish.

Eliza's Sausage Plate

Serves 8

This dish has given me nothing but pleasure. I love butchering meat and throwing in some spices and herbs and developing something wonderful. From the flavors to the cooking methods, its always a learning experience. When grinding meat, keep it very cold to preserve the emulsification. At 221 we freeze our grinders and grind the meat over bowls of ice. When butchering the various meats, leave as much of the fat on as possible, as this will make for a moist sausage. I'm sorry I cannot be more specific on cooking times. The feel of cooked sausage is only realized by lots of practice. Cooking times will vary according to the meat's age and how cold it was kept when grinding. When cooking the sausage, put the sheet tray in the oven as far in advance as possible. This will heat the tray and the sausage should sizzle when it hits the rack.

Spicy Pork Sausage

2 pounds boneless pork butt, cubed

2 tablespoons Old Bay seasoning

2 tablespoons Kosher salt

1 teaspoon ground cloves

1 tablespoon cayenne pepper

1 tablespoon ground cumin

1 tablespoon dark chili powder

Sausage Casings (I prefer pork intestines over lamb)

Cranberry Chicken Sausage with Sage

2 pounds boneless, skinless chicken thighs, cubed

½ cup dried cranberries

¼ cup sage leaves

1 tablespoon Kosher salt

Sausage Casings

Duck Mushroom Sausage

2 pounds boneless, skinless duck legs

½ cup dried shiitake mushrooms

1 tablespoon Kosher salt

Sausage Casings

Lamb Sausage Patties

2 pounds boneless leg of lamb

½ cup oregano leaves

¼ cup garlic cloves, chopped

1 tablespoon Kosher salt

1 tablespoon olive oil

2 tablespoons olive oil

1 **Spicy Pork Sausage:** Combine the pork and the spices. Grind the meat through a large holed grinding plate. Regrind the meat through a smaller holed plate. Preheat oven to 300° and place a rack over a sheet tray in the oven. Rinse the sausage casings and run water through the casings. Place the pork in a sausage press and fill one of the casings.

Should you have leftover meat, fill another casing or use for a tasty sausage stuffing. With a paring knife, prick the sausage every 2 inches on both sides. Place the sausage on the rack and cook for 30 minutes. Flip the sausage and cook for 20-30 minutes or until it is firm. Cool the sausage. It will keep for 5 days refrigerated.

2 **Cranberry Chicken Sausage with Sage**: Combine the chicken, cranberries, sage and Kosher salt. Grind the meat through a large holed grinding plate. Regrind the meat through a smaller holed plate. Preheat oven to 300° and place a rack over a sheet tray in the oven. Rinse the sausage casings and run water through the casings. Place the chicken in a sausage press and fill one of the casings or as many casings as you have meat. With a paring knife, prick the sausage every 2 inches on both sides. Place the sausage on the rack and cook for 30 minutes. Flip the sausage and cook for 20-30 minutes or until it is firm. Cool the sausage. It will keep for 5 days refrigerated.

3 **Duck Mushroom Sausage**: Combine the duck meat, mushrooms and Kosher salt. Grind the meat through a large holed grinding plate. Regrind the meat through a smaller holed plate. Preheat oven to 300° and place a rack over a pan in the oven. Rinse the sausage casings and run water through the casings. Place the duck in a sausage press and fill one of the casings. Should you have leftover meat, fill another casing or use for a tasty sausage stuffing. With a paring knife, prick the sausage every 2 inches on both sides. Place the sausage on the rack and cook for 20 minutes. Flip the sausage and cook for 20-30 minutes or until it is firm. Cool the sausage. It will keep for 5 days refrigerated.

4 **Lamb Sausage Patties**: Combine the lamb, oregano, garlic and Kosher salt. Grind the meat through a large holed grinding plate. Regrind the meat through a smaller holed plate. Form the lamb into 2 ounce patties. Work the meat in your hands for a minute to warm up the fat. Salt the patties. Place a pan over high heat. Add 1 tablespoon of olive oil to the pan and allow to heat. Place the patties in the pan and sear. Cook on a side for 2-3 minutes or until it is crisp. Flip the sausages and cook them to rare. Cool the sausage. It will keep for 5 days refrigerated.

5 **Preheat oven to 400°**. Divide the remaining olive oil between 2 large pans. Slice the sausages into different shapes, allowing an equal portion for 8 guests. Place the sausage in the pans and into the oven. Heat the sausages for 5-7 minutes or until they are crisp on 1 side. Flip the sausages and return them to the oven. Cook the sausages until they are heated through and crisp. I decorate plates with a bit of honey mustard and the spicy glaze from the Spicy Glazed Scallop recipe. Divide the sausages between the plates and serve. You may also opt for serving the sausages on platters with toothpicks.

Fried Oysters with Bleu d'Auvergne, Pear, Pomegranate Vinaigrette & Praline Bacon

Serves 8

This is a wonderful example of how contrasting flavors come together in harmony. If you cannot find pomegranate vinegar, substitute 2 tablespoons red wine vinegar and 2 tablespoons pomegranate juice. The bacon is cooked at a lower heat to allow the sugar to caramelize on the surface.

Pomegranate Vinaigrette

1 shallot, peeled and chopped

¼ cup pomegranate infused vinegar

½ cup olive oil

½ cup extra virgin olive oil

Praline Bacon

½ cup pecans

½ cup brown sugar

11 strips center cut bacon

Fried Oysters

¾ cup cornmeal

1 cup all-purpose flour

2 tablespoons Old Bay seasoning

1 quart canola oil

1 ½ pounds shucked large oysters

1 cup buttermilk

½ pound Bleu d'Auvergne or other high quality blue cheese, rind removed

1 pound mixed greens

2 pears, sliced thinly

1 **Pomegranate Vinaigrette**: In a blender, combine the shallot, pomegranate vinegar, olive oil and extra virgin olive oil. Blend the vinaigrette until it is smooth. The vinaigrette will keep for 1 week refrigerated.

2 **Praline Bacon**: Preheat oven to 325°. In a food processor, combine the pecans and brown sugar. Purée the ingredients until they form a coarse meal. Slice the bacon strips into thirds. Coat one side of the bacon strips with the pecan mixture. Place the coated bacon strips on a parchment lined baking sheet. Place the bacon in the oven and cook for 15 minutes or until the bacon is crisp. Keep a close eye on the bacon as burnt praline bacon is a shame.

Parmigiano Reggiano Baked Chesapeake Oysters:

Here is a quick oyster dish. As a tribute to my Virginia upbringing, I prefer Chesapeake Oysters. Feel free to substitute your favorite oyster. This is also a great hors d'oeuvre but make sure the shells are cool enough to handle before you start handing them out.

Preheat oven to 400°. Rinse and scrub the dirt off of your favorite dozen oysters and shuck them. Place the oysters on a sturdy baking sheet. Spoon 1 teaspoon of cream onto the surface of each oyster. Sprinkle a bit of tarragon over the oysters and top with 2 teaspoons grated Parmigiano Reggiano. Place the oysters into the hot oven for 5-7 minutes or until they are hot and bubbly. Serve while still hot.

3 **Fried Oysters**: In a bowl, whisk together the cornmeal, flour and Old Bay seasoning. Transfer the dredge to a high sided tray. Place the canola oil in a pot over a high heat. When the oil is hot, reduce the heat to medium. Working in batches, submerge the oysters in the buttermilk. Strain the buttermilk off of the oysters and transfer them to the dredge. Thoroughly coat the oysters in the dredge. Fry as many oysters as will fit in your pot of hot canola oil, without crowding the pot. Fry the oysters until they are crisp, about 3-4 minutes. Transfer the oysters to paper towels to remove any excess grease. Sprinkle the oysters with Kosher salt and keep them warm as you fry the rest.

4 **Slice the Bleu d'Auvergne into cubes** and place in a bowl with the greens. Add as much vinaigrette as will just coat the greens and toss in the pears. Place 4 slices of warm bacon on 8 plates. Top the bacon with the warm oysters and top with the greens. Serve to hungry guests.

Peach & Chevre Stuffed Squash Blossoms with Spicy Tomatillo Coulis

Serves 8

Squash blossoms enjoy a short season in the summer. They are very fragile and tough to find. A wonderful farmer, named Hungry, brings me wonderful specimens. The Chipolte chilies give the coulis a hint of smokiness.

Spicy Tomatillo Coulis

2 tablespoons olive oil

1 large yellow onion, chopped

2 cups tomatillos, husks removed and chopped

2 garlic cloves, smashed

2 Chipolte chilies

2 cups chicken stock or water

Peach and Chevre Stuffed Squash Blossoms

1 cup finely diced peaches

½ cup finely sliced scallions

1 cup chevre

½ cup cream cheese

24 squash blossoms

Tempura Batter

3 extra large eggs

1 cup cornstarch

1 tablespoon sesame oil

4 cups all-purpose flour

4 cups cold water

1 quart canola oil

1 **Spicy Tomatillo Coulis**: Place a pot over a high heat. Add the olive oil to the pot and heat until it shimmers. Add the onion with a pinch of salt and reduce the heat to medium. Sauté the onions until they are translucent. Add the tomatillos and garlic to the onions and continue to sauté until the tomatillos are mushy, about 15 minutes. Add the chilies and the stock and simmer for 10 minutes. Blend the sauce and keep it warm.

2 **Peach & Chevre Stuffed Squash Blossoms**: In a mixing bowl, fitted with the paddle attachment, place the peaches, scallions, chevre and cream cheese. Mix the ingredients until they are well incorporated. Very carefully, remove the stamen from the squash blossoms. Using a piping bag, pipe a blossom two-thirds full of filling. Wrap the tips of the petals over the top of the filling. Repeat with the remaining blossoms.

3 **Tempura Batter**: Preheat oven to 300°. Whisk together the egg, cornstarch, sesame oil, flour and water. Set the Tempura Batter aside. Place the oil in a pot over a high heat. Once the oil is hot, reduce the heat to medium. You may test the oil by adding a cube of bread. If the cube browns, your oil is hot. Working in batches, dip a blossom into the tempura batter. Allow any excess batter to drip off of the blossom. Carefully drop the blossom into the hot oil and allow it to fry until golden. Add as many more blossoms as the pot will comfortably hold. You will need to fiddle with the pot's heat to keep the fry oil hot. Sprinkle salt over the blossoms while they are hot. Keep the fried blossoms warm in the oven while cooking the rest. Ladle a bit of sauce onto 8 warm plates. Divide the blossoms between the plates and serve.

Fried Calamari with Jalapeño Tartar

Serves 8

I try to take this off the menu and guests request it again and again. Now that I've revealed the recipe, maybe I could prepare squid differently. I love the tartar in the recipe. It is also great on a simple chicken sandwich. The tartar requires making an emulsification of egg yolks and oil, also called a mayonnaise. If making a mayonnaise is frightening, skip it and replace the yolks and olive oil with 2 cups of mayonnaise. Some like the squid rings to be sliced thickly so it's more of a finger food. I leave this decision up to you. It may seem silly to put the squid in the buttermilk and then squeeze it out. We need a thin layer of the buttermilk or the crust will be clumpy.

Jalapeño Tartar

140 grams pasteurized egg yolks or 7 yolks

2 cups olive oil

1 cup yellow onion, chopped

¼ cup parsley leaves

1 cup canned jalapeños, excess juice squeezed out and reserved

¼ cup jalapeño juice

Dredge

1 ¾ cups cornmeal

2 cups all-purpose flour

2 tablespoons Old Bay Seasoning

1 quart canola oil

2 pounds squid, tubes and tentacles, cleaned and sliced

2 cups buttermilk

1 **Jalapeño Tartar**: In the food processor, place the egg yolks. With the machine running, slowly add 1 ½ cups of the olive oil. Turn off the machine and add the onion and parsley. Start the machine and slowly add another ½ cup of olive oil. Add 1 cup of jalapeños and ¼ cup jalapeño juice and process until combined but still chunky. This will keep refrigerated for 2 weeks.

2 **Dredge**: In a bowl whisk together the cornmeal, flour and Old Bay seasoning and place in a pie tin or high sided platter. Place the canola oil in a pot over high heat. When the oil is hot, reduce the heat to medium. Place the squid in the buttermilk. Squeeze as much of the buttermilk out as possible. Transfer the squid to the dredge and coat thoroughly. The calamari should have a thin coating of dredge, so it is crispy and not bready. Working in batches, fry the squid until it is crisp, about 3-4 minutes. You may need to fiddle with the heat to keep the oil hot. Salt the squid and serve with the Jalapeño Tartar on the side.

Bresaola Wrapped Beef Tips with Olive Pesto

Serves 8

This is a great way to use the scraps of a beef tenderloin. Bresaola is air-cured beef tenderloin. It is more salty than flavorful and gives this dish a beef on beef presentation. You may substitute dried beef but it will be more salty then flavorful. If you can find sundried olives, the flavor surpasses that of regular brined olives. At least use a high quality olive. White anchovies are much more expensive and tastier than those brown specimens.

Olive Pesto

1 cup pitted black olives, sundried or Kalamata

3 garlic cloves, smashed

2 tablespoons fresh basil, chopped

3 tablespoons red pepper, chopped

1 teaspoon ground black pepper

4 anchovy filets, white if possible

1 tablespoon capers

¼ cup Parmigiano Reggiano, finely grated

¼ cup olive oil

Bresaola Wrapped Beef Tips

1 ½ pounds beef tenderloin, trimmed of any fat or sinew

½ pound bresaola, sliced thinly

2 tablespoons olive oil

1 **Olive Pesto**: In the food processor or blender, place the olives, garlic cloves, basil, roasted red pepper, black pepper, anchovy filets and capers. Purée the ingredients until they are smooth. With the machine running, add the olive oil. Transfer the pesto to a squeeze bottle. This will keep, refrigerated for 2 weeks.

2 **Bresaola Wrapped Beef Tips**: You may substitute dried beef for the bresaola in a pinch but it won't be nearly as good. Cutting against the grain, slice the beef into ¾-ounce portions. Wrap each beef tip in a bresaola slice. If the slices are not sticking, your bresaola may be a bit too thick. Brush the bresaola with a lightly beaten egg white and that will help it to adhere to the beef. Place a large pan over a high heat. Add half of the olive oil to the pan and heat until it shimmers. Working in batches, add some beef tips and brown on all sides. Cook the beef tips to your desired doneness and keep warm. Add more oil as needed and brown the remaining beef. Squirt a bit of olive pesto on 8 plates. Top the pesto with the beef tips and serve.

Maine Mussels Steamed in Coconut Milk, Sake, Roasted Red Pepper, Scallion & Cilantro

Serves 8

We receive mussels every Wednesday from Maine. They are dug up on Monday, sent to us on Tuesday and we clean and sell them on Wednesday. 221 has a special every Wednesday. You may have either a bowl of mussels or a bowl of gumbo and a martini or glass of house wine for $15. On this evening we just steam the mussels with white wine, tomato and garlic but if we have any mussels left over, this is one of the preparations we do. Prince Edward Island mussels may be substituted but I prefer Maine bivalves. When chopping cilantro, don't be afraid of the stems as they contain more flavor than the leaves. This is not true of all herbs, as parsley stems are fibrous and bitter.

5 pounds Maine mussels	2 tablespoons unsalted butter	¼ cup scallions, chopped
1 can coconut milk	¼ cup roasted red pepper, chopped	¼ cup cilantro, chopped
½ cup sake, white wine may be used in a pinch		

1 **Pick over the mussels** and discard any that have cracks or holes. Ensure that all of the mussels are closed or close after a good tapping. Remove the beard from the mussels and wipe down with a damp, clean towel. Remove barnacles by scrubbing the mussels with a clean abrasive sponge. If you plan on keeping the mussels for a day, place them in a colander. Cover the colander with ice and place it over a bowl to catch melting ice. Put the colander in the fridge until you are ready to use the mussels. Use the mussels within 48 hours.

2 **Place in a large pot with high sides** the mussels, coconut milk, sake, butter and red pepper. Cover the pot and place it over a high heat. Steam the mussels until they open completely. Add the scallions to the pot. Divide the mussels between 8 warm bowls and sprinkle the cilantro over top.

Red Wine Braised Kobe Short Rib Ravioli with Walnut, Bleu d'Auvergne & Arugula Ravioli

Serves 12

The blue cheese and nuts in this recipe contrast each other nicely. They also provide a flavor that is completely opposite from the rich flavor of the red wine braised short ribs. This is a complicated recipe but well worth the effort.

Red Wine Braised Kobe Short Rib

2 cups red wine

1 onion, chopped

1 leek, white part only, chopped

1 carrot, chopped

1 celery stalk with no leaves, chopped

2 garlic cloves, smashed

2 pounds boneless short rib, Kobe if possible

2 tablespoons olive oil

2 cups veal stock

Pasta

8 extra large eggs

2 egg yolks

1 tablespoon Kosher salt

2 tablespoons extra virgin olive oil

7 cups all-purpose flour

1 cup cornmeal

Walnut, Bleu d'Auvergne and Arugula Ravioli

1 cup toasted walnuts

1 cup Bleu d'Auvergne or other high quality blue cheese, rind removed

1 cup arugula

2 tablespoons truffle oil

1 **Red Wine Braised Kobe Short Rib:** Place the red wine, onion, leek, carrot and garlic into a pot. Place the pot over a high heat and bring the mixture to a boil. Once the mixture has boiled, cool it completely. Trim the short rib of any fat or sinew. Place the short rib into the cooled red wine mixture and allow to marinate overnight.

2 **Preheat oven to 375°.** Take the short ribs out of the red wine marinade and pat them dry with paper towels. Reserving the liquid and vegetables, strain the liquid from the vegetables. Place a wide pot over a high heat. Add the olive oil to the pot and heat until it shimmers. Salt the short ribs and brown them in the hot oil on all sides, about 10 minutes. Transfer the browned beef to a tray and add the strained vegetables to the pot. Sauté the vegetables until they begin to soften. Layer the pan bottom with the vegetables and top with the short ribs. Add the wine to the pot and bring to a boil. Add the veal stock to the pot and bring to a boil. Tightly cover the pot with foil and place in the oven. Allow the meat to cook or braise for 3 hours. Take a piece of short rib out and test to see if it is tender. Test by inserting a fork, if it comes out easily, the meat is done. If the meat is not tender, recover it and place it back in the oven. Retest in another 30 minutes and every 30 minutes after until the meat is tender. Transfer the meat to a container and strain the braising liquid over the meat. Chill the meat in the braising liquid overnight.

3 **Pasta**: Place half the eggs and olive oil in a food processor with half the Kosher salt. Run the machine and add half the flour. Knead the ball of dough for 5 minutes or until it is soft and pliable. Wrap the dough in plastic. Repeat with the remaining ingredients to produce a second ball of dough and allow the balls of dough to rest for 1 hour.

4 **Take the meat out of the braising liquid and reserve the liquid**. It will be the consistency of gelatin. Break the meat up into small chunks and chill until ready to use. Roll one ball of the pasta dough to the thinnest setting. Lay half the dough on a flat surface. Using a 1 ounce scoop, place balls of short rib filling on the dough, leaving 2 inches between each filling. Brush the spaces between the fillings with water. Drape the second sheet of pasta over the first.

Form a tight seal between the 2 layers of pasta and be sure to not have any air bubbles. Cut shapes out of the dough with a pasta cutter. Place ½ cup of the cornmeal on a tray and top with the ravioli. Chill the ravioli. They will keep for 24 hours chilled.

5 **Walnut, Bleu d'Auvergne and Arugula Ravioli**: In a food processor, place the walnuts, Bleu d'Auvergne and arugula. Coarsely chop the ingredients. Chill the filling until ready to use. Roll the second ball of dough as the first. Using a 1 ounce scoop, place balls of walnut filling on the dough, leaving 2 inches between each filling. Brush the spaces between the fillings with water. Drape the second sheet of pasta over the first. Form a tight seal between the 2 layers of pasta and be sure to not have any air bubbles. Cut shapes out of the dough with a pasta cutter. Place the remaining cornmeal on a tray and top with the ravioli. Chill the ravioli. They will keep for 24 hours chilled.

6 **Bring 2 gallons of water to a boil**. Bring the braising liquid to a boil and keep warm. Retrieve 8 of each ravioli from the refrigerator. Working in batches, add the ravioli to the boiling water and cook through, about 5-7 minutes. Place the truffle oil in a bowl. Transfer the cooked ravioli to the oiled bowl and toss to coat. Keep the ravioli warm and repeat the cooking process with the remaining ravioli. Place 1 of each ravioli in a warm bowl. Ladle some hot braising liquid over the ravioli and serve.

Soups

Soup is a complex concoction and when making soups, I layer my flavors. When you taste one of my soups, the flavor changes in your mouth. It may start with Sherry, then progress to butternut squash with a hint of leek, then to the richness of the cream and ending with the hint of thyme. These recipes call for serving the soup straight away. If you can chill the soup and serve it the next day, the flavors will marry and the soup will be more savory. The first six soups are all components in our duo of soups. Here the guest receives two soups in one bowl. We pour the soups in at the same time and then have a decorative swirl in the center. All of these soups are also wonderful by themselves.

Butternut Squash Soup

Serves 8

Roasting the squash ahead of time makes this soup easy and gives it a smoky flavor. When reducing the liquids, stir the pot often. The butternut squash can fall to the bottom and scorch easily.

2 large butternut squash
3 tablespoons olive oil
2 yellow onions, chopped
2 leeks

1 6-inch piece of butcher's twine
2 thyme sprigs
1 ½ cups sherry

1 cup white wine
1 quart chicken stock or water
2 cups heavy whipping cream
chopped chives(optional)

1 **Preheat the oven to 375°.** Slice the squashes, making 2 identical halves. Using a large spoon, scoop out the seeds. Oil a baking sheet with 1 tablespoon of the oil or line a baking sheet with parchment paper. Place the squash cut side down on the baking sheet and roast until soft, about 1 hour. Cool the squash. Once it is cool enough to handle, scoop out the roasted flesh. It will be easier to scoop if it is still a bit warm.

2 **Heat a wide pot over a high heat.** Add the remaining olive oil to the pot. When the oil is hot, add the onion with a pinch of salt. The salt will draw the liquid out of the onion. Stir the onion with a wooden spoon or heat safe spatula and reduce the heat to medium. Cook the onion until it is translucent, about 10 minutes. While the onion is cooking, prepare the leeks. Cut the root and the green leaves off of the leeks. Reserve 1 large green

leaf. You should be left with the white and light green shafts. Slice the shafts down the middle and run under cool water. The layers of the leek should be free of dirt. Chop the leek. When the onion is translucent, add the leeks. Cook the leeks for about 5 minutes. Add the roasted and scooped butternut squash and stir to heat through.

3 **Wrap the reserved green leek leaf** around the thyme and secure the package, or bouquet garni, with the butcher's twine. Add the bouquet garni to the vegetables. Stir the soup frequently. Add the sherry and white wine and simmer for 5 minutes. Add the stock to the vegetables and reduce by half. Add the cream and simmer the soup for 10 minutes, stirring frequently. Working in batches, blend the soup. Place the soup in a clean pot and heat until it bubbles. Serve the soup in warm bowls garnished with chopped chives, if you like.

Cauliflower Soup

Serves 8

This is a simple soup. The richness of the cauliflower and the cream is contrasted by the prosciutto. Prosciutto is the cured leg of a hog. As you slice closer to the hoof, the slices become less desirable. Ask your butcher if he has an end piece of prosciutto he wants to be rid of.

2 tablespoons olive oil

2 yellow onions, chopped

pinch of Kosher salt

2 leeks

1 head of cauliflower, core removed and chopped

¼ pound of prosciutto, preferably an end piece and unsliced

1 quart chicken stock or water

1 cup heavy whipping cream

1 **Heat a wide pot over a high heat.** Add the olive oil to the pot. Add the onion with a pinch of Kosher salt and reduce the heat to medium-high. The salt will draw the liquid out of the onion. Stir the onion with a wooden spoon or heat safe spatula and reduce the heat to medium. Cook the onion until it is translucent, about 10 minutes. While the onion is cooking, prepare the leeks. Cut the root and the green leaves off of the leeks. You should be left with the white and light green shafts. Slice the shafts down the middle and run under cool water. The layers of the leek should be free of dirt. Chop the leek. When the onion is translucent, add the leeks and cauliflower. Cook the vegetables until they are soft. If your prosciutto is sliced, tie it in cheese cloth. Add the prosciutto and the stock to the vegetables and reduce by half.

2 **Add the cream to the soup** and reduce by one-quarter. Discard the prosciutto. Working in batches, purée the soup until it is smooth. Return the soup to a clean pot and heat until it bubbles. Ladle the hot soup into eight bowls and serve immediately.

Kale Soup with Apple Smoked Bacon

Serves 8

Great for a cold and dreary winter day, the kale has a touch of bitterness that is complimented well with the smoky, salty bacon.

1 pound apple smoked bacon	2 carrots, peeled and chopped	2 cups heavy whipping cream
1 tablespoon olive oil	1 large red pepper, seeded and chopped	2 bunches green curly kale
2 yellow onions, chopped		
2 leeks	1 quart chicken stock or water	

1 **Slice the bacon into thick matchsticks.** In a wide pot over a medium-high heat, place the bacon. When the bacon begins to sizzle, reduce the heat to medium-low and cook until the bacon is crisp, about 10-15 minutes. With a slotted spoon, transfer the bacon to paper towels.

2 **Drain off all but 2 tablespoons of bacon fat**. Add the onion with a pinch of Kosher salt and increase the heat to medium. The salt will draw the liquid out of the onion. Stir the onion with a wooden spoon or heat safe spatula and be sure to scrape all of the brown bits of protein off of the pot's bottom. Cook the onion until it is translucent with brown edges, about 15 minutes. While the onion is cooking, prepare the leeks. Cut the root and the green leaves off of the leeks. You should be left with the white and light green shafts. Slice the shafts down the middle and run under cool water. The layers of the leek should be free of dirt. Chop

the leek. When the onion is translucent, add the leeks, carrots and red pepper. Cook the vegetables until they are soft. Add the stock to the vegetables and reduce by half.

3 **While the soup is reducing**, place 2 quarts water and 2 tablespoons Kosher salt over a high heat. Bring the water to a boil. Rip the kale leaves off of their stalks and plunge them in the pot of boiling water. Blanch the kale for 3-4 minutes or until it is bright green. Plunge the kale in a bowl of ice water and leave it there until it is completely cool. Strain the kale and squeeze out any excess liquid.

4 **Add the cream to the soup** and reduce by one-quarter. Remove the soup from the heat. Working in batches, purée the soup with the kale until it is smooth. Return the soup to a clean pot and heat until it bubbles. Divide the cooked bacon between eight bowls. Ladle in the hot soup and serve immediately.

Spicy Carrot Soup with Ginger

Serves 8

The carrots, jalapeño and ginger work together to make a fabulous soup. If you really like the spice, add another jalapeño. Feel free to use this to steam open some clams or mussels and finish the dish with a bit of cilantro and chopped scallions.

2 tablespoons olive oil

2 yellow onions, chopped

2 leeks, light green and white parts only, washed free of dirt and chopped

1 large red pepper, cored, seeded and chopped

7 carrots, peeled and chopped

3 garlic cloves, peeled and smashed

1 2-inch knob of ginger, peeled and chopped

1 fresh jalapeño, chopped

2 cups sake or dry white wine

1 quart chicken stock

2 cups heavy whipping cream

1 **Heat a wide pot over a high heat.** Add the olive oil and reduce the heat to medium-high. Add the onion with a pinch of Kosher salt. Sauté the onion until it is translucent, about 7-9 minutes. Add the leeks, red pepper, carrots, garlic and jalapeño. Cook the vegetables until they are soft and fragrant, about 10 minutes.

Increase the heat to high and add the sake to the vegetables. Bring the sake to a boil and reduce by half. Add the chicken stock to the pot and reduce by half. Add the cream to the pot and reduce by 1/3rd. Working in batches, blend the soup until it is smooth. Reheat the soup in a clean pot and ladle into 8 warm bowls.

Six Herb Pea Soup with Cilantro Cream

Serves 8

This soup explodes in the mouth with fresh flavor. The mint tends to take the starring role with basil lending strong support and the allium family bringing up the rear. This soup is enjoyable chilled.

Six Herb Pea Soup

2 tablespoons olive oil

2 yellow onions, chopped

pinch of Kosher salt

3 bunches scallions

1 1-inch knob of ginger, peeled and chopped

2 leeks, light green and white parts only, washed free of dirt and chopped

1 quart chicken stock or water

1 cup heavy whipping cream

1 cup flat leaf parsley leaves

1 cup fresh mint leaves

1 cup fresh basil leaves

1 cup chives

4 cups peas, fresh or frozen

Cilantro Cream

1 cup sour cream

1 bunch cilantro

juice of 2 limes

1 **Cilantro Cream**: Blend sour cream with the lime juice and the cilantro. Transfer to a squeeze bottle. This will keep refrigerated for 1 week.

2 **Six Herb Pea Soup**: Heat a wide pot over a high heat. Add the olive oil and reduce the heat to medium-high. Add the onion with the salt. Sauté the onion until it is translucent, about 10 minutes. Chop the scallions keeping the white and the green parts separate. When the onions are translucent, add the white part of the scallions, the ginger and the leeks and cook the vegetables until they are soft, about 10 minutes. Add the chicken stock to the pot and reduce by half. Add the cream to the pot and reduce by half. Set the soup aside.

3 **While the soup is reducing**, bring 2 quarts of water to a boil with 2 tablespoons of Kosher salt. Plunge the parsley, mint, basil and chives into the pot of boiling water. Blanch the herbs until they are bright green, about 3-5 minutes. Plunge the herbs in ice water and cool completely. Strain the water out of the herbs and squeeze out any excess liquid. Bring the water back to a boil and plunge the peas into the boiling water. Blanch the peas until they are bright green. Transfer the peas to ice water and cool completely. Once the peas are cool, strain them. Bring the soup to a boil. Add the strained peas and bring the soup to a boil again. Remove the soup from the heat. Working in batches, blend the soup with the herbs. This will keep for 5 days refrigerated.

4 **Reheat the Six Herb Pea Soup** and serve with the Cilantro Cream and some Fried Sweet Potatoes.

Creamy Mushroom Soup
with Truffle Oil

Serves 8

This soup is earthy and warming. Sometimes I'll use the soup as a sauce on a hearty fish or steak dish. You may choose to garnish the soup with a cooked shiitake cap as I have in the photo.

2 tablespoons olive oil

2 yellow onions, chopped

pinch of Kosher salt

2 leeks

2 cups crimini mushrooms, cleaned and chopped

2 cups shiitake mushrooms, cleaned, stemmed and chopped

2 cups oyster mushrooms, cleaned, stemmed and chopped

2 thyme sprigs

1 6-inch piece of butcher's twine

2 cups red wine

1 quart chicken stock or water

1 cup heavy whipping cream

Truffle Oil

1 Heat a wide pot over a high heat. Add the olive oil to the pot. When the oil is hot add the onion with a pinch of Kosher salt. The Kosher salt will draw the liquid out of the onion. Stir the onion with a wooden spoon or heat safe spatula and reduce the heat to medium. Cook the onion until it is translucent, about 10 minutes. While the onion is cooking, prepare the leeks. Cut the root and the green leaves off of the leeks. Reserve 1 large green leaf. You should be left with the white and light green shafts. Slice the shafts down the middle and run under cool water. The layers of the leek should be free of dirt. Chop the leek. When the onion is translucent, add the leeks. Cook the leeks for about 5 minutes. Add the 3 types of mushrooms and cook until they have released their liquid, about 10 minutes.

2 Wrap the reserved green leek leaf around the thyme and secure the package, or bouquet garni, with the butcher's twine. Add the bouquet garni to the vegetables. Add the red wine and reduce by half. Add the stock to the vegetables and reduce by half. Add the cream and reduce the soup by 1/3rd. Working in batches, blend the soup. Return the soup to a clean pot and heat until it bubbles. Serve the soup in warm bowls garnished with truffle oil.

Olathe Corn Bisque with Smoked Trout

Serves 8

This is a lovely summer soup. Olathe, Colorado produces incredible sweet corn. In recent years, some of the farmers have opted not to raise the edible varieties but focus on the strains for ethanol. This makes this corn even more of a treasure. I really enjoy the sweetness of bisque that can only be had with a shellfish stock or fumet. It's important not to overcook the stock as the delicate broth just loses its flavor. Traditional French methods dictate that you must blend the shells with the cooked vegetables, strain and discard the solids and then add the liquid to a blond roux. I prefer to make the shrimp stock and then add it to the vegetables with cream and then blend the vegetables. The result is a not as rich soup. Please do not substitute canned corn as the result is a tinny tasting concoction.

Fumet

1 tablespoon olive oil

2 pounds shrimp shells

2 bay leaves

Corn Bisque

2 tablespoons olive oil

2 yellow onions, chopped

2 leeks, light green and white parts only, washed free of dirt and chopped

2 cups white wine

2 cups heavy whipping cream

8 ears of fresh corn or 3 cups frozen corn

1 pound smoked trout filet

1 **Fumet**: Place a pot over a high heat. When the pot is hot, add the olive oil and heat the oil until it shimmers. Add the shrimp shells, bay leaves and a pinch of Kosher salt. Heat the shells until they begin to turn pink. Add enough water to just cover the shells. Bring the stock to a boil and reduce the heat to medium. Simmer the stock for 25 minutes. Strain the shells and bay leaves out of the stock and reserve the liquid.

2 **Corn Bisque**: Heat a wide pot over a high heat. Add the olive oil to the pot and heat until it shimmers. Add the onion with a pinch of Kosher salt. Reduce the heat to medium-high and cook the onions until they are translucent, about 8-10 minutes. Add the leeks to the pot and cook them for 10 minutes or until they are limp. Increase the heat to high and add the white wine to the pot. Reduce the wine by half. Add the shrimp stock to the pot and reduce by half. Add the cream to the pot and reduce by half.

3 **While your bisque is reducing**, husk the corn and remove any silks. Cut the corn off of the cobs. Run the back of your knife against the cobs to release any milk. Reserve 1 cup of cut corn kernels. Add the remaining corn and its milk to the reduced soup and allow it to heat through. I find if you bring the bisque to a boil, at this point, then the corn turns brown and chewy, so just heat the corn. Working in batches, blend the bisque until it is smooth. Return the bisque to a clean pot and bring it to a simmer. Flake the trout and remove any pin bones. Divide the trout and corn kernels between 8 hot bowls. Ladle the hot bisque into the bowls and serve.

Chilled Cucumber Soup with Smoked Salmon

Serves 8

This is lovely for a summer luncheon with a dry white wine. I don't get many takers for this here in the San Juan Mountains but it remains one of my summer catering selections.

6 large cucumbers	2 tablespoons champagne vinegar	1 pound cold smoked salmon, thinly sliced
10 scallions	¼ cup mint leaves	Mint leaves (optional)
2 cups plain yogurt		

1 **Chill 8 soup bowls**. Peel the cucumbers and slice them lengthwise, forming identical halves. With a spoon, scoop out the seeds. Roughly chop the cucumbers. Remove the root from the scallions. Finely chop the scallions. Working in batches, blend the cucumbers, scallions, yogurt, vinegar and mint. Blend until smooth and divide between 8 chilled soup bowls. Roll the salmon slices into cylinders. Slice the cylinders, making ribbons out of the salmon. Divide the salmon between the soup bowls and garnish with mint leaves.

Cucumber

The cucumber is a tasty treat in spring and summer. English cucumbers can be easier, as they are seedless. They're also a great choice as an hor d'oeuvre base, as their thin skin does not require peeling. When buying cucumbers, choose firm specimens and avoid puffy or shriveled ones. Don't buy cucumbers that are yellowing or with bruises and soft spots. A light sauté in butter with salt and plenty of pepper, makes a great side to grilled chicken. In the U.S. we consume most of our cucumbers raw or pickled.

White Bean Soup with Garlic Roasted Leg of Lamb

Serves 8

This soup is perfect for a cold evening, of which we have a lot in Telluride. The soup is better if you let it sit overnight, making it a three day affair, but if you can't wait then by all means dig in. As with the Cauliflower Soup, this requires a scrap of prosciutto. Your butcher should have an end piece he does not want. In most of my soups, I start the vegetables with a pinch of Kosher salt. Not in this case. Salt could harden beans and halt the cooking process. With this soup, we add the salt at the end. The age of your beans dictates the cooking time. The older the bean, the longer it takes for it to soften. As the beans cook, they may soak up more than the listed amount of chicken stock. The overnight soak of the beans should prevent this but add more stock or water as needed.

White Bean Soup

4 cups white beans, Cannelini or Great Northern

2 tablespoons olive oil

1 large yellow onion, finely diced

2 leeks, light green and white parts only, washed free of dirt and finely diced

2 carrots, peeled and finely diced

6 cups chicken stock

1 prosciutto end piece

Garlic Roasted Leg of Lamb

10 garlic cloves

2 tablespoons olive oil

¼ cup fresh oregano leaves

2 pounds leg of lamb

1 **White Bean Soup**: Pick any stones out of the beans and place the beans in a bucket. Add enough cold water to cover 3 inches above the beans. Refrigerate the beans overnight. Strain the water out of the beans. Heat a wide pot over a high heat. Add the olive oil and heat until it shimmers. Add the onion and reduce the heat to medium-high. Cook the onion until it is translucent, about 10 minutes. Add the leek and carrot. Continue to cook the vegetables until they are soft, about 10 minutes. Add the beans to the pot and stir to combine. Add the chicken stock and stir to combine. Add the prosciutto end. Allow the stock to come to a boil and reduce the heat to medium. Keep the soup at a strong simmer until the beans are soft, about 2-3 hours. Stir the soup occasionally. When the beans are tender, transfer ¼ of the soup to the blender. Blend the soup until it is smooth and return it to the pot with the remaining soup. If chilling overnight, leave the prosciutto in the soup until ready to reheat.

The Great Lamb Debate: Domestic vs. New Zealand

There are many good reasons to use both types of lamb. New Zealand lamb has dined upon some of the best and greenest grass in the world, producing their gamy flavor. They also have plenty of room to roam in this vast country. Although lamb from the states do not have the same high quality feed and less room, in some cases they produce a less fatty product,. Due to domestic lamb's shorter travel time, it is easier on Mother Earth and a fresher product. I suggest using domestic when in need of fresh product and New Zealand when using frozen lamb.

2 **Garlic Roasted Leg of Lamb**: Preheat oven to 400°. Toss the garlic cloves in 1 tablespoon of the olive oil and place in a small pan with a pinch of Kosher salt. Tightly cover the garlic and roast it until it is soft, about 15 minutes. Cool the garlic. While the garlic is roasting, trim any tendons or sinew from the lamb and score any fat. With a sharp knife, score the inner layer of the lamb. Combine the cooled garlic with the oregano and 1 tablespoon Kosher salt. Add the garlic mixture to the scored, inner layer of the lamb and tuck the garlic into the creases. Roll the leg up and secure with butcher's twine. Generously salt and pepper the lamb. Place an oven safe pan over high heat. When the pan is hot, add the remaining olive oil and heat until it shimmers. Add the lamb to the pan and brown it on all sides, about 10 minutes. Transfer the pan to the oven and continue to cook it to your desired doneness. Depending on the size and age of your meat, 5 minutes for rare, 10 for medium-rare and 15 for medium. Any more cooking than that and you'll loose the wonderfully gamey flavor of the lamb.

Allow the meat to rest, loosely covered for 5 minutes. You could chill the lamb and use it the next day. Remove the prosciutto from the soup. Reheat the bean soup over a medium-high heat and stir often. Do not try to speedily heat up the soup over a high heat. The beans will stick to the bottom and burn. Remove any twine from the lamb and thinly slice it. Ladle the hot soup into 8 warm bowls. Top the soup with the lamb and serve.

Spicy Gumbo with Chicken & Sausage

Serves 8

I came very close to forgetting this treat. Guests ask me for the recipe all the time. It has a big kick of cayenne so be careful. File, or ground sassafras leaves, is a traditional spice in gumbo.

4 chicken legs

3 tablespoons olive oil

2 yellow onions, finely diced

2 red peppers, seeds and white membrane removed and finely diced

10 celery stalks, leaves removed and finely diced

1 tablespoon Old Bay Seasoning

1 teaspoon File

1 teaspoon ground cumin

1 tablespoon dark chili powder

3 teaspoons cayenne pepper

3 ounces unsalted butter

3 ounces all-purpose flour

1 quart chicken stock

1 pound pork sausage, sliced

2 cups cooked white rice

1 **Preheat the oven to 375°.** Toss the chicken legs in 1 tablespoon of the olive oil and place on a baking sheet. Generously salt the chicken legs and place in the oven. Cook the legs until they are cooked through, about 45 minutes. Chill the legs completely. When they are cool enough to handle, pick the meat off of the bones and give it a rough chop.

2 **Heat a wide pot over a high heat.** Add 2 tablespoons of the olive oil to the pot. When the oil is hot add the onion with a pinch of Kosher salt. The Kosher salt will draw the liquid out of the onion. Stir the onion with a wooden spoon or heat safe spatula and reduce the heat to medium. Sauté the onion until it is translucent, about 10 minutes. Add the peppers and celery and cook until they are soft, about 10 minutes. Add the Old Bay seasoning, File, cumin, chili powder and cayenne pepper. Cook until the spices are fragrant, about 5 minutes. Spoon the vegetables out of the pot and reduce the heat to low. Melt the butter in the pot and whisk in the flour. Increase the heat to medium and constantly whisk the flour and butter until they are dark brown, about 10-15 minutes. Return the vegetables to the pot and stir to combine. Carefully, whisk the chicken stock into the vegetables. Bring the Gumbo to a simmer. Stirring occasionally, simmer the Gumbo for 1 hour. Add the chicken meat and sausage to the pot and allow to heat through. Ladle the Gumbo into 8 hot bowls and top with a bit of white rice.

Lentil Soup with Prosciutto Chips

Serves 8

A warming soup with lots of cumin kick. What did the spice cabinet say to the knocking salesman? You can knock but you can't cumin. You may opt to not serve the Prosciutto Chips. The soup is more than able to stand alone but the Prosciutto Chips lend flavor and texture. When making the Prosciutto Chips, keep a close eye as burnt prosciutto is not nearly as tasty.

Lentil Soup

2 tablespoons olive oil

1 small onion, finely chopped

pinch of Kosher salt

3 celery stalks, leaves removed and finely chopped

2 carrots, peeled and finely chopped

2 garlic cloves, peeled and finely chopped

1 tablespoon cumin

1 teaspoon coriander

1 teaspoon dark chili powder

3 cups lentils

5 cups chicken stock or water

Prosciutto Chips

2 tablespoons olive oil

6 thin slices of prosciutto

1 **Lentil Soup**: Heat the olive oil in a wide pot over a medium-high heat. Add the onion and pinch of Kosher salt. Cook the onion until it is translucent, about 10 minutes. Reduce the heat to medium and add the celery and carrots. When the vegetables are soft stir in the garlic, cumin, coriander and chili powder and cook for an additional 3 minutes.

2 **Rinse the lentils under cold water** and pick out any stones. Add the lentils and chicken stock to the pot. Place the pot over a high heat and stir to release any spice crust from the bottom and sides of the pot. When the liquid comes to a boil, reduce the heat to medium and simmer the lentils until they are tender, about 2-3 hours.

If the lentils appear to be drying out, add water as needed. Cooking time depends on the type of lentils used as well as their age. Older lentils will take longer to cook.

3 **Prosciutto Chips**: Turn the oven to 400°. Spread the olive oil onto a baking sheet. Place the prosciutto on the oiled baking sheet and put it in the oven. Cook the prosciutto until it is crisp, about 5 minutes. Transfer the prosciutto to paper towels to remove any excess grease. Break the slices into large fragments.

4 **Blend 2 cups of the soup until smooth.** Return this liquid to the lentils and heat until the soup bubbles. Divide the Lentil Soup between eight bowls and top with Prosciutto Chips.

Salads

Many of my salads are dressed with simple vinaigrettes. I prefer a bit of oil and vinegar as opposed to heavy, creamy dressings. A bit of acid brings out the true flavor of the greens. Mix and match these dressings for your own creation. You will notice that all of my vinaigrettes are made with a blend of extra virgin olive oil and olive oil. I feel the flavor of extra virgin olive oil tends to be strong and overwhelming. The flavor is great for dipping with bread or drizzling over vegetables but I like the olive oil to play a supporting role in the salad. As with sauces and soups, dressings benefit from being made the day before serving. This allows the flavors to mingle and develop. This is especially true of the Caesar Dressing recipe.

Salads are a great forum for showing off cheeses in their natural state. When heating a cheese, the flavor changes. A tangy Bleu d'Auvergne, a creamy Chevre or nutty Manchego work well with greens and vinaigrettes.

Organic Mixed Greens with Sherry Vinaigrette, Golden Beets, Haystack Chevre & Candied Pecans

Serves 8

This salad changes with every season. This was the version in the summer of 2008. Our green salads have a balance of flavors and textures. I find the balance works best with nuts, fruit, cheese and a flavorful vinaigrette. Please do not attempt to dress this salad long before it is served. The greens will wilt and it will turn into salad soup. If you'd like to set out the salads ahead of time, offer the vinaigrette on the side. Haystack Chevre is made in Boulder, CO and has won a few awards.

Roasted Beets

3 medium sized golden beets

Sherry Vinaigrette

4 garlic cloves

¾ cup + 1 tablespoon olive oil

¾ cup extra virgin olive oil

½ cup sherry vinegar

1 teaspoon Dijon Mustard

Zest of 1 lemon

Candied Pecans

nonstick spray

3 tablespoons corn syrup

2 tablespoons granulated sugar

¾ teaspoons Kosher salt

½ teaspoon coarsely ground black pepper

1 ½ cups pecans

1 ½ pounds mixed greens

½ cup Chevre

1 **Roasted Beets**: Preheat oven to 400°. Wash the beets and place in a pan, covered tightly with foil. Cook until the beets are tender, about 45 minutes to an hour depending on the size of your beets. Cool the beets slightly. While the beets are still warm, wrap a beet in a dish towel. Rub the beet until the skin falls off. This trick only works with warm beets. If you allow your beets to cool too much, remove the skin with a peeler or paring knife. Repeat with the remaining beets. Cut the beets into thin wedges and chill.

2 **Sherry Vinaigrette**: While the beets are cooking, place the garlic cloves with 1 tablespoon of olive oil and a pinch of Kosher salt into a pan. Tightly cover the pan and place into the oven. Roast the garlic cloves until they are soft, about 15 minutes. Blend until smooth the roasted garlic, sherry vinegar, Dijon mustard, lemon zest, olive oil, extra virgin olive oil and Kosher salt and pepper to your liking. Set the vinaigrette aside. If not using straight away, refrigerate. This vinaigrette will keep for 2 weeks refrigerated.

Other great green salad accoutrements:

- Pear, Manchego, Pine Nuts and Rosemary Vinaigrette

- Grape, Fennel, Comté with Parsley Vinaigrette

- Pink Grapefruit, Almond, Chevre with Balsamic Vinaigrette

- Peach, Feta, Walnut with Champagne Vinaigrette

- Bleu d'Auvergne, Apple, Hazelnut and Apple Cider Vinaigrette

- Grilled Baby Zucchini, Halloumi, Figs and Pomegranate Vinaigrette

- Daikon, Carrot, Blood Orange Sections, Sesame Seeds and Rice Wine Vinaigrette

- Roasted New Potatoes, Bacon and Dijon Vinaigrette

3 **Candied Pecans:** Preheat oven to 350°. Spray a baking sheet with nonstick spray. Whisk together the corn syrup, sugar, Kosher salt and pepper in a bowl. Add the pecans; stir gently to coat. Transfer the nuts to baking sheet. Bake pecans for 5 minutes. Using a fork, stir pecans to coat with melted spice mixture. Continue baking until pecans are golden and the coating bubbles, about 10 minutes. Take the nuts out of the oven. Working quickly, separate nuts with a fork and then cool. If the nuts are not separated while hot then they become one large piece of candy instead of a lightly coated nut.

4 **Toss the greens** with as much Sherry Vinaigrette as you wish. Neatly line the Roasted Beet slices on 8 chilled plates. Top the Roasted Beets with the dressed greens. Top the greens with the Candied Pecans and crumble the Chevre over the salads. Serve the salads immediately.

Caesar Salad with Parmigiano Reggiano, Croutons & White Anchovies

Serves 8

The secret to 221's Caesar Salad is that we use high quality white anchovies. You may substitute the brown slimy things from a can but if you can find the white filets, you will be much happier. If you've never made an emulsification of egg yolks and oil before, you may have a period of failure. If your mixture is not thick or thickening, it may have broken and you'll need to start again. With the many ingredients, this emulsification is difficult. You may want begin with the Lemon Aioli recipe later in this chapter. You will have guests that will not eat the whole anchovy on their plate. Gently persuade them to try a little bite. It will open their senses to a whole new world. You will have extra dressing but it won't be a problem to get rid of.

Caesar Dressing

140 grams of pasteurized egg yolks or 7 fresh yolks

1 heaping teaspoon Djion mustard

2 tablespoons chopped garlic

2 cups extra virgin olive oil

2 cups olive oil

¼ cup lemon juice

¼ cup red wine vinegar

2 tablespoons Worcestershire Sauce

¼ cup white anchovies, excess juice squeezed out

¾ cup Parmigiano Reggiano, finely grated

1 tablespoon freshly ground black pepper

Croutons

3 cups cubed, day-old french bread

¼ cup olive oil

3 hearts of romaine

½ cup Parmigiano Reggiano, finely grated

8 whole white anchovies

1 **Caesar Dressing**: Place pasteurized yolks in a standing mixer with the Dijon mustard and the garlic. Set the mixer on high and mix until the yolks are frothy. Separately, combine the oils. Reduce the mixer speed to medium high and slowly drizzle half of the oil mixture into the yolks until thick. In a separate bowl, mix together the lemon juice, red wine vinegar and Worcestershire sauce. Reduce the mixer speed to medium and add half of the lemon juice mixture.

Slowly add half of the remaining oil mixture. Add the remaining lemon juice mixture. Place the ¼ cup of anchovies into a food processor. Process the anchovies until they are smooth. Reduce the mixer speed to low and add the puréed anchovies in 3 batches. Add the grated Parmigiano Reggiano and black pepper and stir until combined. Transfer the dressing to a container and refrigerate.
The dressing will keep for 1 week, chilled.

Parmigiano Reggiano

Parmigiano Reggiano is a wonderful treat that has been produced for 800 years. Much of the flavor comes from the unpasteurized milk used to produce it. The cows and what they consume must come from the Parmigiano Reggiano district. One-thousand liters of early morning milk goes into 60 kg of Parmigiano Reggiano. An average wheel weighs 75-90 pounds whereas domestic Parmesan weighs 24 pounds. The Italian version is less salty than domestic Parmesan because the large wheels do not get as saturated with salt during brining. Parmigiano Reggiano's long aging produces a complex flavor and texture. The characteristic crunch of Parmigiano Reggiano stems from the proteins breaking down into free amino acid crystals during the latter half of the aging process. The crystals are visible as white dots.

2 **Croutons**: Preheat oven to 375°. Toss the cubed bread with the olive oil and add Kosher salt and pepper to your liking. Spread the bread cubes onto a baking sheet. Bake the croutons until they are golden brown, about 10 minutes. Please use a timer as burnt croutons do not make for a good snack. Cool the croutons.

3 **Wash and dry the romaine hearts**. Rip or cut the hearts into bite size pieces. Toss the lettuce in as much dressing as you prefer. Divide the dressed lettuce between 8 chilled plates. Place the croutons around the plate, if the croutons are still warm that is a bonus for your guests. Sprinkle the grated Parmigiano Reggiano over the salads and top with the whole anchovies. Serve the salads.

Rock Shrimp Slaw with Tangy Dressing, Panko Crusted Tiger Shrimp & Fried Capers

Serves 8

I love to alter this salad at the beginning of each season and my regular guests will tell me the old one was better. Hopefully by giving my guests the ability to make this dish, I can become a bit more creative with my shrimp salad. Should you have leftover dressing, it makes a great dip for vegetables or fried foods. The caper is a bud that will flower. By frying the buds we force them into a flower and a crispy, salty flower at that.

Tangy Dressing

100 grams pasteurized or 5 fresh egg yolks

1 heaping tablespoon prepared horseradish

¾ cup olive oil

½ cup ketchup

2 tablespoons Worcestershire sauce

Rock Shrimp

1 ½ pounds small rock shrimp

½ head green cabbage

¼ head red cabbage

1 large carrot, peeled

Panko Crusted Tiger Shrimp

8 large tiger shrimp, peeled and deveined

8 thin ½-inch slices of ginger

½ cup all-purpose flour

½ cup panko breadcrumbs

2 eggs, lightly beaten with 1 teaspoon water

Fried Capers

3 cups canola oil

½ cup capers

1 **Tangy Dressing**: Place the egg yolks and horseradish in a standing mixer. Set the machine to high and mix the yolks until they are frothy. Reduce the machine's speed to medium high and slowly drizzle in half of the olive oil. Reduce the mixer's speed to medium and add the ketchup and Worcestershire sauce. Increase the mixer's speed to medium-high and slowly add the remaining olive oil. Transfer the dressing to a container and chill. The dressing will keep for 1 week refrigerated.

2 **Rock Shrimp**: Place 1 quart of water and 1 tablespoon of Kosher salt in a pot over a high heat. When the water comes to a boil, add the rock shrimp. Cook the rock shrimp until firm, about 7 minutes. Strain the boiling water from the shrimp and run them under cold water until they are completely cool. Chill the Rock Shrimp until ready to use.

3 **With a slicer or sharp knife**, core and thinly slice the cabbages. Place the cabbages in a large bowl. Slice the carrots into thin matchsticks and toss into the cabbage. Set the cabbage mixture aside until ready to use.

4 **Panko Crusted Tiger Shrimp**: Using a toothpick, adhere a slice of ginger to each tiger shrimp. Place the flour and panko into separate pie tins. Lightly coat the shrimp with the flour. Transfer the shrimp to the egg mixture. When the shrimp are covered in egg, transfer them to the panko and dredge the shrimp in the panko. Chill the shrimp until ready to use.

5 **Fried Capers**: Place the canola oil in a pot over a high heat. When the oil is hot, reduce the heat to medium. Rinse the capers under cold water and pat dry. Capers that are not rinsed, make a very salty end result. Being very careful of the splatter, place the capers in the hot oil and fry them until they open, about 3 minutes. If your capers do not open, they will be soggy as opposed to crispy. Use a fine stainer to fish the capers out of the hot oil. Transfer the capers to paper towels, thereby removing any excess grease. Increase

the heat of the oil to medium-high. Add one Panko Crusted Tiger Shrimp to the pot of oil. If the shrimp floats, then your oil is sufficiently hot. If it sinks, then remove it and wait for the oil to heat. Working in batches, fry the Panko Crusted Tiger Shrimp until golden brown, about 5-7 minutes. Remove any excess grease by transferring the shrimp to paper towels. Keep the Panko Crusted Tiger Shrimp warm.

6 **Add the Rock Shrimp to the cabbage**. Add as much Tangy dressing as you prefer and toss to combine. Divide the dressed cabbage and Rock Shrimp among 8 chilled plates. Sprinkle the Fried Capers around the plates. Remove the toothpicks from the Panko Crusted Tiger Shrimp and place the shrimp atop the cabbage. Serve immediately. Should you need a pot luck or picnic dish, this is great without the fried shrimp. The cabbage will stay crisp under the dressing for hours.

Peekytoe Crab Salad with Lemon Aioli, Champagne Vinaigrette & Pink Grapefruit

Serves 8

Peekytoe Crab is a breed of crab found all along the east coast but are most abundant in Maine. They weigh less than a pound and their flesh is delicate and sweet. A simple presentation of the crab is the best method. Be careful not to handle the crabmeat too much, you'll break up those lovely lumps. Tobiko is flying fish roe and comes in a rainbow of flavors and colors. It adds a wonderful texture of tiny bursting pellets. When using, add just a touch so as not to overwhelm the other flavors.

Lemon Aioli

80 grams pasteurized egg yolks or 4 fresh egg yolks

½ cup olive oil

3 tablespoons lemon juice

Champagne Vinaigrette

½ cup champagne vinegar

¾ cup olive oil

¾ cup extra virgin olive oil

1 shallot, peeled and chopped

Peekytoe Crab Salad

2 pink grapefruit

1 ½ pounds peekytoe crabmeat

2 tablespoons tobiko

2 tablespoons chives

½ pound mixed greens

1 **Lemon Aioli:** Place the egg yolks in the bowl of a standing mixer. Set the mixer on high and mix the yolks until they are frothy, about 2 minutes. Reduce the speed to medium-high. Slowly drizzle in half of the olive oil. Add the lemon juice. Slowly drizzle in the remaining olive oil. Refrigerate the aioli. This will keep chilled for 2 weeks.

2 **Champagne Vinaigrette:** In a blender, combine the vinegar, olive oil, extra virgin olive oil and shallot. Blend the ingredients until they are smooth. Salt and pepper the vinaigrette to your liking. Transfer the vinaigrette to a container. If not using straight away then chill. It will keep chilled for 1 week.

3 **Peekytoe Crab Salad:** With a sharp knife, cut the rind away from the grapefruit. With a sharp paring knife, slice the grapefruit sections away from the pith. Remove any seeds or white pith from the grapefruit sections.

4 **In a bowl combine the Peekytoe crab**, tobiko, chives and as much lemon aioli as you prefer. Carefully mix the ingredients. Lightly coat the mixed greens in the vinaigrette. Divide the greens among 8 chilled plates. Decoratively arrange the grapefruit sections on the plates. Top the greens with the crab and serve.

Citrus Cured Salmon Salad with Shaved Fennel

Serves 8

Wild salmon is much preferred in this dish. The acidic flavor of the zests, complements the rich salmon perfectly. Should you not have the 48 hours for the salmon to cure, simply slice the salmon thinly and sprinkle the cure over it. After 30 minutes the result will be the same. Add some extra flavor with some orange sections on the plate.

Citrus Cured Salmon

zest of 1 orange

zest of 1 lime

zest of 1 lemon

½ cup brown sugar

½ cup Kosher salt

1 ½ pounds wild salmon, skin and pin bones removed

2 tablespoons black pepper

Shaved Fennel

2 fennel heads

2 tablespoons orange juice

½ cup extra virgin olive oil

1 **Citrus Cured Salmon**: In a bowl, combine the zests, brown sugar, Kosher salt and black pepper. Press the cure onto the salmon and wrap the salmon in cheesecloth. Place the salmon in a perforated pan or colander set over a bowl. Place a plate on the salmon and a 1 pound weight on the plate. Weight the salmon for 24 hours. Flip the salmon and weight for an additional 24 hours. Wipe any cure off of the salmon and thinly slice. If your knife isn't sharp enough to do the trick, simply place the salmon in the freezer for 30 minutes. The salmon will firm up and be easier to slice.

2 **Shaved Fennel**: Chop ¼ cup of fennel fronds from the heads. Place the chopped fronds into a bowl. Remove any stalks or cores from the fennel heads. Thinly slice the fennel heads and add to the fronds. Add the orange juice and extra virgin olive oil to the fennel and generously salt and pepper. Toss the fennel until it is coated. Lay the salmon slices on 8 chilled plates. Place a ball of fennel in the center of the plates and serve.

Shaved Cabbage with Balsamic Vinaigrette, Pine Nuts & Bleu d'Auvergne

Serves 8

This is an incredibly simple salad from our vegetarian menu. Feel free to dress this salad up to an hour in advance of serving because the cabbage just soaks up dressing and makes it more flavorful. It's a perfect twist on traditional cole slaw for picnics. Bleu d'Auvergne is a cow's milk cheese from the French Alps. It is extremely creamy and dreamy.

Balsamic Vinaigrette

½ cup Balsamic vinegar

¾ cup olive oil

¾ cup extra virgin olive oil

½ cup pine nuts

Shaved Cabbage

½ head white cabbage

¼ head red cabbage

1 large carrot, peeled

¾ cup Bleu d'Auvergne or other high quality blue cheese, rind removed

1 **Balsamic Vinaigrette**: Whisk together the vinegar and oils. Salt and pepper to your liking. If not using straight away, refrigerate. This vinaigrette will keep for a month refrigerated.

2 **Preheat oven to 375°**. Spread the pine nuts onto a baking sheet. Roast the nuts until they are warm and fragrant, about 5 minutes. Have a timer, it is such a shame to burn such expensive nuts. Set the pine nuts aside to cool.

3 **Shaved Cabbage**: On a slicer or with a very sharp knife, core and thinly slice the cabbages. Slice the carrot into thin matchsticks and add it to the cabbage. With tongs or your hands toss the cabbage, carrot and pine nuts. Add as much vinaigrette as you prefer and toss to combine. Divide the cabbage between 8 chilled plates, sprinkle the toasted pine nuts around the cabbage and crumble the Bleu d'Auvergne over. Serve the salads.

Pineapple, Chevre & Basil Salad with Spicy Miso Dressing & Macadamia Nuts

Serves 8

This is listed as a salad but is also a great salsa on grilled fish. The vinaigrette is spicy but the pineapple dilutes the spice nicely. The spice of the jalapeño lies in its seeds and membranes. The more care you take in removing these white pieces, the less spice you'll have.

Spicy Miso Dressing

½ cup white miso paste

1 fresh jalapeño

½ cup honey

½ cup water

zest of 1 lime

2 tablespoons lime juice

2 tablespoons sesame oil

2 tablespoons soy sauce

2 tablespoons fresh chopped ginger

1 cup olive oil

½ cup macadamia nuts

1 pineapple, peeled and diced

½ cup fresh basil chopped

½ cup chevre

1 **Spicy Miso Dressing**: In a blender, combine the miso, jalapeño, honey, water, zest, lime juice, sesame oil, soy sauce and ginger. Blend the ingredients until they are smooth. With the machine running, slowly add the olive oil. Chill unless using straight away. This will keep refrigerated for 2 weeks.

2 **Preheat the oven to 375°**. Spread the macadamia nuts onto a baking sheet. Roast the nuts until they are slightly brown and aromatic, about 5 minutes. Please keep a timer on these nuts as they are very expensive and burn easily. Cool the nuts completely.

3 **In a bowl, combine** the macadamia nuts, pineapple and basil. Dress the fruit with as much Spicy Miso Dressing as you like and divide between 8 chilled plates. Crumble the chevre over the salads and serve. I usually garnish with a fried basil leaf but there is no reason to heat up the oil for just a garnish.

Haricot Vert Salad with Herb Dressing, Tomato Petals, Arugula & Citrus Honey Vinaigrette

Serves 8

Mistakes are my inspiration. This salad was an inspiration when I ordered too much haricot vert. Frozen or canned haricot vert just does not work in this case. The crunch of the fresh beans is imperative.

Tomato Petals

10 roma tomatoes

3 garlic cloves, peeled and smashed

1 thyme sprig

2 basil sprigs

2 cups olive oil

Herb Dressing

½ cup sour cream

2 tablespoons red wine vinegar

10 chives

1 tablespoon heavy whipping cream

¼ cup parsley leaves

Citrus Honey Vinaigrette

½ cup orange juice

2 tablespoons honey

1 shallot, peeled and chopped

1 cup olive oil

1 pound haricot vert, trimmed

1 pound arugula

1 **Tomato Petals**: Preheat the oven to 250°. Place 2 quarts of cold water and 2 tablespoons of Kosher salt in a pot over a high heat. Core the tomatoes and mark the bottoms with an "X". Working in batches plunge the tomatoes into the boiling water. Blanch the tomatoes until their skin begins to flay off, about 5-7 minutes. The time will vary according to the ripeness of your tomatoes. Transfer the tomatoes to an ice bath and cool completely. When the tomatoes are cool, scrape the skins off with a paring knife. Quarter the tomatoes and remove any seeds or membranes. Place the tomatoes in a pan with the garlic, thyme, basil and olive oil. Roast the tomatoes for 2 hours or until they are fragrant. Cool the tomatoes in the oil. Refrigerated in oil, these will keep for 2 weeks.

2 **Parsley Dressing**: In a blender, place the sour cream, red wine vinegar, chives, cream and parsley. Blend the ingredients until they are smooth. Transfer to a container and chill. This will keep for 1 week, refrigerated.

3 **Citrus Honey Vinaigrette**: In a blender, combine the orange juice, honey, shallot and olive oil. Blend the ingredients until they are smooth. If not using straight away, transfer to a container and chill. This will keep for 2 weeks, refrigerated.

Tomatoes

This summer fruit tastes wonderful alone and complements any dish. The best tomatoes appear at the end of summer. In the market, choose tomatoes that are firm, smooth, pleasant smelling and free of bruises. Refrigerate tomatoes only to chill them. Refrigeration tends to diminish tomatoes' flavor and soften their texture. Tomatoes are best left on a window sill to ripen.

Tomatoes are low in sodium and rich in vitamins A and C. Tomatoes also supply potassium and folic acid. This fruit acts as a diuretic and a mineralizer. Tomatoes stimulate the appetite, combat scurvy and cleanse the system of toxins. Tomatoes are a major source of lycopene, which is a substantial antioxidant and anticancer agent.

4 **Place 2 quarts of cold water** and 2 tablespoons of Kosher salt in a pot over a high heat. When the water comes to a boil, add the haricot vert. Blanch the haricot vert until they are bright green but still crisp. Plunge the haricot vert into an ice bath. Cool the haricot vert completely. Strain the ice water off of the beans and pat dry. Slice the haricot vert into ½ -inch pieces.

5 **Place the Tomato Petals in a warm place** for 1 hour before using, to melt the oil. Fan the Tomato Petals on 8 chilled plates. Toss the haricot vert in as much of the Herb Dressing as you like. Place the dressed haricot vert in the center of the Tomato Petals. Dress the arugula in as much of the Citrus Honey Vinaigrette as you wish and place the arugula on top of the haricot vert. Serve the salads with a lovely Sauvignon Blanc.

Belgian Endive with Toasted Walnuts, Bleu d'Auvergne & Parsley Vinaigrette

Serves 8

Belgian Endive grows beneath the soil's surface. This is how it remains nice and white with no chlorophyll to tarnish its appearance. Cut the endive just before you're about to serve it. Otherwise the edges turn a horrible brown color and no amount of lemon juice will prevent it. The bitterness of the endive leaves complements the nuts and the creamy cheese well. It is a nice surprise if the nuts are still warm when you serve the salads.

Parsley Vinaigrette

½ cup flat leaf parsley leaves

2 tablespoons honey

1 shallot, peeled and chopped

½ cup champagne vinegar

¾ cup olive oil

¾ cup extra virgin olive oil

1 cup walnuts

10 Belgian endive heads, any brown leaves removed

½ pound Bleu d'Auvergne or other high quality blue cheese, rind removed

1 **Parsley Vinaigrette**: Place a pot with 1 quart of cold water and 1 tablespoon of Kosher salt over a high heat. When the water comes to a boil, add the parsley leaves. Cook the parsley until it is bright green, about 2-3 minutes. Transfer the parsley to ice water and cool completely. Squeeze any excess liquid out of the parsley and place the leaves in a blender with the honey, shallot, champagne vinegar, olive oil and extra virgin olive oil. Blend the vinaigrette until it is smooth. This vinaigrette is best used the day it is made, to preserve its bright green color. Refrigerated the vinaigrette will keep for 1 week but will darken.

2 **Preheat the oven to 375°.** Spread the walnuts onto a tray and place in the oven. Toast the walnuts until they are slightly brown and aromatic, about 5 minutes. Please have a timer on your walnuts and check them often. Walnuts that are even just a bit charred are bitter.

3 **Remove 40 of the larger leaves** and place them decoratively on 8 chilled plates. Core the remaining endive and slice the heads into thin long strips. Toss the strips in as much Parsley Vinaigrette as you prefer. Divide the dressed endive between 8 chilled plates. Crumble the Bleu d'Auvergne over the salads and top with the warm walnuts. Drizzle a bit of the Parsley Vinaigrette around the plate for decoration and serve.

Watermelon, Peach, Blueberry, Red Onion & Feta Salad with Balsamic Vinaigrette

Serves 8

A refreshing salad that is great for picnics. This is also a great salsa for shrimp tacos.

Balsamic Vinaigrette

½ cup Balsamic vinegar

¾ cup olive oil

¾ cup extra virgin olive oil

1 red onion,
papery skin removed

1 quart canola oil

½ cup buttermilk

1 cup all-purpose flour

1 tablespoon
Old Bay Seasoning

4 cups diced seedless
watermelon, no rind

2 cups diced peaches

2 cups blueberries

1 cup Feta cheese

1 **Balsamic Vinaigrette**: Whisk together the vinegar, olive oil and extra virgin olive oil. Salt and pepper to your liking. This will keep refrigerated for 1 month.

2 **With a slicer or a very sharp knife**, thinly slice the red onion into rings. Place the canola oil in a pot over a high heat. When the oil is hot, reduce the heat to medium. Cover the onion rings with the buttermilk. Whisk together the flour and Old Bay Seasoning and place it in a pie tin. Working in batches, lift the onion rings out of the buttermilk and let the excess buttermilk drip off. Transfer the onion rings to the flour and coat the onion rings thoroughly. Shake off any excess flour and place the onion rings on a tray. Working in batches, fry the onion rings until they are crisp, about 4-6 minutes. Carefully lift the onion rings out of the oil and liberally salt. Keep the onion rings in a warm area.

3 **In a bowl, combine** the watermelon, peaches, blueberries, Feta and as much dressing as you desire. Toss the fruit. Divide the fruit between 8 chilled plates and top with the warm onion rings.

Petite Salad with Mixed Greens, Fig Lemon Vinaigrette, Prosciutto Wrapped Asparagus, Zucchini Tempura & Sweet Garlic Pickles

Serves 8

I started doing this salad about 5 years ago and it's still my favorite. I wanted to combine different culinary aspects on one plate. The asparagus is Italian, the Tempura is Japanese and Garlic Pickles are Eastern European. Feel free to enjoy all three of these items separately.

Sweet Garlic Pickles

1 tablespoon coriander seed

3 garlic cloves, smashed and peeled

3 cups rice wine vinegar

¼ cup granulated sugar

¼ cup Kosher salt

2 chili d'arbols, or other dried chili

2 cucumbers, sliced

1 red pepper, seeds and membrane removed and thinly sliced

Fig Lemon Vinaigrette

½ cup fig-lemon balsamic vinegar

¾ cup olive oil

¾ cup extra virgin olive oil

Prosciutto Wrapped Asparagus

2 bunches asparagus

8 thin slices of prosciutto

½ cup fresh mozzarella, cut into 8 thick match sticks

1 tablespoon olive oil

Zucchini Tempura

3 extra large eggs

1 cup cornstarch

1 tablespoon sesame oil

4 cups all-purpose flour

4 cups cold water

1 quart canola oil

2 zucchini, sliced on the bias into 16 pieces

½ cup sweet chili sauce

1 pound mixed greens

1 **Sweet Garlic Pickles**: Using the bottom of a pot or the side of your knife, lightly crush the coriander seeds. Place in a pot, the coriander seeds, garlic, vinegar, sugar and salt. Crush the chilies in your hands and add them to the pot. Bring the mixture to a boil and boil until the sugar and salt have dissolved. When smelling this concoction, do not put your nose directly over the pot, rather waft some of the steam your way. Direct vinegar fumes can harm your sinuses. Pour the vinegar mixture over the cucumbers and red pepper. Cover tightly, refrigerate and brine for at least 3 days. These will keep for 1 month, refrigerated.

2 **Fig Lemon Vinaigrette**: Whisk together the vinegar and olive oils. Salt and pepper to your liking. Set the vinaigrette aside. If not using straight away, refrigerate. This vinaigrette will keep for a month refrigerated.

3 **Prosciutto Wrapped Asparagus:**
Bring 2 quarts of water to a boil with 2 tablespoons of Kosher salt. Remove the woody stems from the bottoms of the asparagus spears by bending each spear until it snaps. Plunge the spears into the boiling water. Allow the asparagus to cook for 5-7 minutes or until the spears are bright green and tender. Transfer the spears to an ice bath and cool completely. Strain the ice water from the asparagus and pat the spears dry. Lay 1 prosciutto slice on a clean surface. Place 2 pieces of asparagus on an end of the prosciutto. Top the asparagus with a mozzarella slice. Top the cheese with 2 additional pieces of asparagus. Roll the prosciutto tightly around the asparagus and cheese. Repeat until you have 8 prosciutto wrapped asparagus. Place a large pan over a high heat. When the pan is hot, add the olive oil and heat until it shimmers. Add the asparagus wraps to the pan and brown on all sides, about 7-9 minutes. Transfer the asparagus to paper towels to remove any excess grease and keep the wraps warm.

4 **Zucchini Tempura:** Whisk together the egg, cornstarch, sesame oil, flour and water. Set the tempura batter aside. Place the oil in a pot over a high heat. Once the oil is hot, reduce the heat to medium. You may test the oil by adding a cube of bread. If the cube browns, your oil is hot. Working in batches, dip a zucchini slice into the tempura batter. Allow the tempura batter to drip off a bit and place the zucchini in the hot oil. Fry the zucchini until it is crisp and golden, about 4-6 minutes. Transfer the zucchini to paper towels to remove any excess grease and salt liberally. Repeat this process with the remaining zucchini adjusting the canola oil's heat as necessary.

5 Toss the greens in as much of the vinaigrette as you prefer. Divide the greens between 8 chilled plates. Place a prosciutto wrapped asparagus on each plate. Squirt a bit of sweet chili sauce on each plate and top with 2 pieces of zucchini tempura. Place 3 pickle slices on each plate. Serve the salads.

Tuna Tartare with Avocado Mash, Citrus Ginger Vinaigrette, Fried Gyoza Skins & Arugula

Serves 8

When you purchase a loin of tuna you receive a gift of beautiful meat that is wonderful raw or seared rare. You also receive quite a bit of sinew. Take a spoon and scrape the meat from the sinew. You must serve the tuna immediately as the sesame oil turns the dish a brown color. I use a combination of sesame oil and extra virgin olive oil on the tuna, as sesame oil can overpower the natural flavor of the tuna. If you plan on making the Avocado Mash ahead of time, leave the pits in as they keep it from turning black.

Citrus Ginger Vinaigrette

½ cup orange juice

2 tablespoons honey

2 scallions, chopped

2 tablespoons chopped, fresh ginger

1 garlic clove, smashed and peeled

1 cup olive oil

Avocado Mash

4 avocados

juice of 2 limes

zest of 1 lime, finely chopped

¼ cup scallions, finely chopped

¼ cup cilantro, chopped

Crisp Gyoza Skins

3 cups canola oil

16 gyoza or wonton wrappers

Tuna Tartare

1 ½ pounds sashimi grade Ahi Tuna, finely chopped

¼ cup toasted sesame seeds

2 tablespoons sesame oil

2 tablespoons extra virgin olive oil

½ pound arugula

1 **Citrus Ginger Vinaigrette**: In a blender, combine the orange juice, honey, scallions, ginger, garlic and olive oil. Blend the ingredients until they are smooth. Transfer to a container and chill, if not using straight away. This will keep for 2 weeks, refrigerated.

2 **Avocado Mash**: In a bowl, mash together the avocados, lime juice, zest, scallion and cilantro. Chill if not using straight away.

3 **Crisp Gyoza Skins**: Place the canola oil in a pot over a high heat. When the oil is hot, reduce the heat to medium. Working in batches, fry the gyoza wrappers until they are crisp. If you flip them half way during the cooking process, it should only take 3-5 minutes. Transfer the wrappers to paper towels to remove any excess grease and liberally Kosher salt them. Cool the crisp gyoza skins.

4 **Tuna Tartare**: In a bowl, combine the tuna, sesame seeds, sesame oil and extra virgin olive oil. Salt and pepper the tuna to taste. Dress the arugula with as much Citrus Ginger Vinaigrette as you wish. Place a spoonful of Avocado Mash on a chilled plate. Top the Avocado Mash with a Crisp Gyoza Skin. Top the Crisp Gyoza Skin with 2 tablespoons of Tuna Tartare. Top the Tuna Tartare with a Crisp Gyoza Skin. Top the Crisp Gyoza Skin with some arugula. Repeat on 7 more plates and serve.

Main Courses

Main Courses are difficult to develop and therefore the most fun. Each component must be flavorful and complex enough to stand on its own but must compliment the other pieces of the dish. I've separated each component into it's own recipe. Most of the recipes are timed so everything finishes together.

I call for a resting time for meat. When cooking a piece of meat, the juices run rapidly through and eventually out of the meat. When slicing into a freshly cooked piece of meat, the juices will continue to run and run out all over your cutting board. By allowing the meat to rest, the juices can slow down and will remain in the meat once sliced. I'm not asking to serve cold meat but the end product will be more juicy and flavorful with a short rest. If your resting area is too cool or the resting period is more that 5 minutes, by all means reheat the meat on a grill for a couple minutes.

All of these dishes are better if served on a warm plate. Think ahead and put your plates in a recently hot oven or turn the oven to 250° and heat your plates for 10-20 minutes. Do not forget to handle your plates with a pot holder and warn your guests of the warm plates.

Potato Crusted Halibut with Asparagus, Fennel Verjus & Garlic Mashers

Serves 8

I learned this recipe while living in Napa Valley. I lived with four other cooks and we were all students at Culinary Institute of America at Greyhead. Our dinner parties were incredible, each cook trying to out do the next. I learned so much in California and it holds a special place in my heart. The Verjus in this recipe with the fennel seed gives the sauce a nutty hint. I do not pepper my mashers, at least not with black pepper as I like the pristine look of white potatoes. Please snap the woody ends off of the asparagus as opposed to cutting them off. Snapping ensures all of the tough fibers have been removed.

Fennel Verjus

2 tablespoons olive oil

2 large yellow onions, chopped

4 small or 3 large fennel bulbs, stalks removed and reserved

2 leeks, white and green parts only, cleaned of any dirt and chopped

¾ cup fennel seed

3 bottles Verjus Blanc, the juice of unripened grapes

Garlic Mashers

1 tablespoon olive oil

7 garlic cloves, peeled and smashed

1 quart heavy cream

5-6 large Yukon Gold potatoes, peeled

4 ounces unsalted butter, cubed

Asparagus

2 bunches asparagus, woody ends snapped off

1 tablespoon butter

½ cup chicken stock

Potato Crusted Halibut

2 ½ pounds halibut filet

¼ cup olive oil

1 Russet potato, peeled

1 **Fennel Verjus**: Place a wide pot over a high heat. When the pan is hot, add the olive oil. Heat the oil until it shimmers. Add the onions and cook them until they are translucent. Stir the onions frequently. Chop the fennel bulbs and stalks and keep separate. Add leeks to the onions and continue to sweat the vegetables. Add the chopped fennel bulbs without the stalks. When translucent, add the fennel seed and stir to combine. Allow the seeds to cook until they are fragrant, about 2 minutes. Add the chopped stalks and stir. Add the verjus and bring to a boil. Top with 3 cups

cold water and bring to a boil. Once the Fennel Verjus has boiled, reduce the heat to medium and simmer for 2 hours. Strain through a fine chinois. Chill and reheat when ready to use. Refrigerated this will keep for 1 week.

2 **Garlic Mashers**: Place a pot over medium heat and add 1 tablespoon olive oil or just enough oil to cover the bottom. Add the garlic and reduce the heat to low. Frequently stirring, cook the garlic until fragrant and add the cream. Lightly simmer the cream until it tastes like garlic, about 20 minutes. Careful not to let the cream boil over because it will make a huge mess. Slice the Yukon Golds and place in a pot. Top with cold water and 1 tablespoon of Kosher salt. Place the pot over a high heat and when it comes to a boil, reduce to a simmer and skim off any foam. Simmer until the potatoes are tender, 45 minutes to 1 hour. Strain the potatoes and reserve a bit of the cooking liquid to ease the milling. Once cooked, if the potatoes are left in hot water the starch will absorb water and make the potatoes less creamy. Food mill the potatoes, adding cooking liquid as needed. Place the milled potatoes in a stainless steel pot with half of the cubed butter. Place the pot over a medium-high heat and constantly stir. Add the remaining butter and then add half the warm garlic cream. Stir until the Garlic Mashers are warm and creamy. You may not need all of the garlic cream but it is great for soups or sauces. Season the Garlic Mashers with Kosher salt and keep warm.

3 **Asparagus**: Place 2 quarts of water with 2 tablespoons Kosher salt over a high heat and bring the water to a rapid boil. Plunge the asparagus into the boiling water and allow to cook for 7-8 minutes or until the spears are tender. The cooking times will vary according to the size and age of your asparagus. Transfer the asparagus to a bowl of ice water and cool completely. Drain the ice water off of the asparagus and place in a pot with the butter, chicken stock and salt and pepper, to your liking.

4 **Potato Crusted Halibut**: Preheat the oven to 400°. Skin the halibut and cut into 8 portions. With a super sharp peeler, peel strips off of the Russet potato. If you're not using them immediately, store in cold water. When ready to cook the halibut, place 2 tephlon pans over a high heat for 30 seconds. Divide the olive oil between the 2 pans or enough oil to come up to ¼ inch height of the pans. Heat the oil until it shimmers and reduce the heat to medium. Kosher salt and pepper the fish to your liking. With you hands, wring as much water as possible out of the peeled potatoes. Top the halibut portions with the Russet potatoes in a thin layer. Place the fish, potato side down in the hot pan and cook until the potatoes are crisp, about 5 minutes. Place the pan in the oven for 5-6 minutes or until the fish is almost cooked through. This cooking time will vary according to the thickness and age of your fish. Flip the fish and finish the cooking on the stove top over medium high heat until cooked through, about 4-5 minutes.

5 **Place the Asparagus over a high heat** and cook until it is hot. Reheat the Fennel Verjus. Heat 8 wide dinner bowls and place a spoonful of hot Garlic Mashers in the center of each. Pour 2 ounces of Fennel Verjus into the bowl and divide the hot Asparagus between the bowls. Top the Asparagus with the Potato Crusted Halibut and serve immediately.

Ruby Red Trout with Squash, Mushroom, Chard Ravioli & Caper Brown Butter

Serves 8

This is a classic preparation of Trout. The Caper Brown butter screams Classic French Cuisine and matches with the fish and the pasta beautifully. This is a dish I've tried to alter and my guests always request its return to the menu. This filling is very easy to work with. It keeps its shape and doesn't ooze out should you have a pin hole in the dough. If you'd like to keep the ravioli for a while, skip the cornmeal and freeze them, spread out on a tray, lined with wax paper.

Squash Mushroom Chard Ravioli

2 large butternut squash

3 tablespoons olive oil

1 bunch red Swiss chard

3 cups chopped mushrooms, shiitake, oyster and crimini

4 extra large eggs

1 egg yolk

2 teaspoons Kosher salt

1 tablespoon extra virgin olive oil

3 ½ cups all-purpose flour

½ cup cornmeal

2 tablespoons truffle oil

Caper Brown Butter

6 ounces unsalted butter

¼ cup lemon juice

¼ cup capers, rinsed

Ruby Red Trout

8 6-ounce portions of skin on red meated trout, pin bones removed

4 tablespoons olive oil

3 tablespoons parsley, chopped

1 Squash Mushroom Chard Ravioli: Preheat the oven to 375°. Slice the butternut squashes lengthwise, producing 2 identical halves. With a spoon, remove any seeds. Rub the squash with 2 tablespoons of the olive oil and place cut side down on a sheet tray. Roast the squash for 1 ½ hours or until it is soft. Allow the squash to cool. When the squash is cool enough to handle, remove the flesh from the skin and cool on a tray.

2 Bring 2 quarts of water to a boil with 2 tablespoons of Kosher salt. Trim any stem off of the chard leaves. Plunge the leaves into the boiling water and allow to cook for 7-8 minutes or until the leaves are tender. Transfer the chard to a bowl of ice water and cool completely. Drain any water off of the chard. Squeeze any excess water from the chard and add the leaves to the butternut squash.

3 Heat a pan over a high heat. Add the remaining olive oil to the pan and heat until it shimmers. Add the mushrooms to the pan with a pinch of salt. Reduce the heat to medium and sauté the mushrooms until they release all of their liquid, about 7-9 minutes. Add the mushrooms to the butternut squash and chard and cool the mixture completely.

4 **Place the eggs, yolk, salt and extra virgin olive oil** in a food processor. Run the machine until the ingredients are combined. Add flour and pulse until it is just combined. Knead the ball of dough for 5 minutes or until it is soft and pliable. Wrap the dough in plastic and allow it to rest for 1 hour.

5 **Salt and pepper** the butternut squash filling to your liking. Roll the pasta dough to the thinnest setting. Lay ½ of the dough on a flat surface. Using a ½ ounce ice cream scoop, place balls of filling on the dough, leaving 3 inches between each filling. Brush the spaces between the fillings with water. Drape the second sheet of pasta over the first and be sure to not have any air bubbles. Cut squares out of the dough with a pasta cutter. Place the cornmeal on a tray and top with the ravioli. Chill the ravioli. They will keep for 24 hours chilled or 1 week frozen. Bring 1 gallon of water to a boil.

6 **Caper Brown Butter**: Place the butter in a pot over a medium-high heat. Allow the butter to melt and then foam. Do not stir the butter. Allow the foam to die down. There should be bits of protein on the bottom of the pan, allow these to brown. When the bottom of the pan is brown and the butter emits a nutty aroma, add the lemon juice and capers. Being careful of the steam, whisk the butter off of the heat. Use your whisk to release any brown bits from the bottom of the pan. Set the sauce aside. Working in batches, add enough ravioli to the boiling water that they have room to cook and are not crowded. Place the truffle oil in a bowl. Allow the ravioli to cook for 5-7 minutes or until they are soft and warm in the center. Transfer the ravioli to the bowl with the truffle oil and toss to coat. Cook the remaining ravioli in the same manner and transfer to the truffle oil bowl. Keep the ravioli warm.

7 **Ruby Red Trout**: Generously salt and pepper the trout filets. Heat 2 large pans over high heats. Heat 1 tablespoon olive oil in each pan until it shimmers. Working in batches, place 2 trout filets, flesh side down, in each of the pans and reduce the heat to medium. Cook the trout for 3-5 minutes and flip to the skin side. Cook the skin side until it is crisp and the fish is cooked through, about 4-6 minutes. Keep the Ruby Red Trout warm. If your fish is a bit under, it will continue to cook as it rests and the hot Caper Brown Butter will finish the cooking process. Add the remaining olive oil to the pans and cook the rest of the trout. Place the Caper Brown Butter over a high heat. When the butter comes to a boil, add the parsley and whisk. Divide the Squash Mushroom Chard Ravioli and Ruby Red Trout between 8 warm plates and pour the sauce over the fish.

Citrus Marinated Tilapia with Corn & Crab Stuffed Artichoke

Serves 8

I love the combination of crab and artichoke. We have all met up with the sub par crab and artichoke dip at cocktail parties. This combination is much lighter and allows the taste of the crab to really shine through. Manchego is a hard sheep's milk cheese that is made in the Spanish Alps. It has a slightly nutty flavor and is a welcome addition to any cheese plate. The sweet flavor of the Tilapia is accentuated by the quick marinade. The short marinade time is due to the thin filet of the Tilapia. Citrus dehydrates fish and will produce a dry filet if marinated too long. The cooking method of the Tilapia may seem a bit involved. The natural sugars in the fruit juices burn easily. By following the stove top-oven-stove top method, we get a nice color on the fish but don't over cook it.

Citrus Marinade

2 lemons

2 oranges

2 limes

¼ cup olive oil

¼ cup honey

Crab and Corn Stuffed Artichoke

8 artichokes

2 lemons, halved

4 ears of corn

¼ cup chopped parsley

2 tablespoons chopped scallions

1 cup Manchego cheese, grated

1 ½ pounds lump crabmeat, picked over

½ cup Parmigiano Reggiano, grated

Tilapia

2 tablespoons olive oil

8 5-6 ounce Tilapia filets

1 **Citrus Marinade**: In a blender combine the zest and juice of the oranges, limes and lemons. Blend with the olive oil and honey. Transfer the marinade to a squeeze bottle. It will keep for a week refrigerated.

2 **Crab and Corn Stuffed Artichoke**: Break the stem off of an artichoke and discard. By breaking the stem off of an artichoke, you remove some of those pesky fibers. If you were to cut the stem off, all of the fibers would remain in the base of the artichoke heart. With a serrated knife, slice the top third of the artichoke off and discard it. Use scissors to trim off any sharp ends of leaves. Rub the cut side of the artichoke with a lemon half. Repeat this process with the remaining artichokes. Place the artichokes in a wide pot with the lemons. Fill the pan with water to half the height of the artichokes. Cover the pot and place it on a high heat. When the steam begins to escape from the covering, reduce the heat to medium and simmer the artichokes for 1 hour or until they are tender. Test the doneness of an artichoke by tugging on one of its leaves. If it comes off easily the artichoke is done. Cool the artichokes.

Artichokes

A member of the thistle family, the artichoke is the flower of a garden plant that developed from the cardoon. A native of the Mediterranean it was highly respected by the Greeks and Romans. The middle ages saw it as an aphrodisiac, thus it became scarce. Catherine de Médicis brought it to France from Italy, where it prospered. It came to California in the 19th century, tucked in the baggage of Italian immigrants. The moist, foggy and temperate climate of Monterey County blossomed artichokes into an important crop of the 1920s.

This vegetable grows on a plant that stands 3-5 feet and has indented leaves. Eat prior to flowering. If the leaves are spread, it is overripe and the choke is tough. Choose specimens that are compact, heavy for their size and tightly packed with bright green leaves. Avoid any with discolored leaves or brown tips as they lack freshness and tend to have a pungent flavor.

The artichoke is an excellent source of potassium, for alertness, and magnesium. It is also a good source of folic acid and supplies vitamin C, copper, iron, phosphorus niacin, vitamin B6, zinc, pantothenic acid and calcium. It may serve as an appetite stimulant, blood cleanser, antitoxin, diuretic and is good for the liver.

3 **Preheat the oven to 400°**. Shuck the ears of corn. Rub the ears with a paper towel or dish towel to remove any silks. Slice the corn off of the cobs. Scrape the cobs with the back of your knife to release any juice or milk. It's easiest if you scrape them right over a bowl. In a bowl combine the corn kernels, corn milk, parsley, scallions and Manchego. Add the crab and toss with a spoon. Be careful not to break up the lumps. With a spoon, remove the center choke from each artichoke. Divide the crab mixture between the artichokes and place them on a baking sheet. Top the artichokes with the Parmigiano Reggiano and bake them in the oven for 15 minutes or until the crab is hot and the top is crispy and brown.

4 **Tilapia**: Place ½ of the citrus marinade in a shallow pan. Add the Tilapia filets and allow to marinate for 10 minutes. Place 2 pans over high heats. Generously Kosher salt and pepper the fish. When the pans begin to smoke, divide the olive oil between the 2 pans and turn off the heat. Place the filets in the pans. Transfer the pans to the oven and cook for 3-5 minutes. Transfer the pans to the stove top. Place the pans over medium heats and flip the filets. Cook until the Tilapia is cooked through, about 3-5 minutes. Divide the artichokes between 8 warm plates. Place a Tilapia filet on each plate and squirt a bit more marinade on each filet. Serve with a light side salad.

Menage a Foie Praline Crusted Foie Gras, Pâté de Foie Gras and Grilled Foie Gras with Ham, PAGE 10

Eliza's Sausage Plate, PAGE 12

Fried Oysters with Bleu d'Auvergne, Pear, Pomegranate Vinaigrette and Praline Bacon, PAGE 14

Fried Calamari with Jalapeno Tartar, PAGE 17

Bresaola Wrapped Beef Tips with Olive Pesto, PAGE 18

Maine Mussels Steamed in Coconut Milk, Sake, Roasted Red Pepper, Scallion and Cilantro, PAGE 19

Red Wine Braised
Kobe Short Rib
Ravioli with
Walnut, Bleu
d'Auvergne and
Arugula Ravioli,
PAGE 20

Butternut
Squash Soup
& Cauliflower
Soup,
PAGES 24 & 25

Kale Soup with
Apple Smoked
Bacon & Spicy
Carrot Soup
with Ginger,
PAGES 26 & 27

Six Herb Pea
Soup with Cilantro
Cream and Fried
Sweet Potatoes,
PAGE 28

Olathe Corn
Bisque with
Smoked Trout,
PAGE 30

Creamy Mushroom Soup
with Truffle Oil, PAGE 29

68

Caesar Salad with Parmigiano Reggiano, Croutons and White Anchovies, PAGE 40

White Bean Soup with Garlic Roasted Leg of Lamb, PAGE 32

Rock Shrimp Slaw with Tangy Dressing, Panko Crusted Tiger Shrimp and Fried Capers, PAGE 42

Pineapple, Chevre and Basil Salad
with Spicy Miso Dressing
& Macadamia Nuts, PAGE 47

Peekytoe Crab Salad
with Lemon Aioli,
Champagne
Vinaigrette
and Grapefruit,
PAGE 44

Haricot Vert
Salad with Herb
Dressing, Tomato
Petals, Arugula
and Citrus Honey
Vinaigrette,
PAGE 48

Belgian Endive with Toasted
Walnuts, Bleu d'Auvergne and
Parsley Vinaigrette, PAGE 50

Watermelon, Peach, Blueberry,
Red Onion and Feta Salad with
Balsamic Vinaigrette, PAGE 51

Petite Salad with Mixed Greens,
Fig Lemon Vinaigrette, Prosciutto
Wrapped Asparagus, Zucchini Tempura
and Sweet Garlic Pickles, PAGE 52

Tuna Tartare with Avocado Mash,
Citrus Ginger Vinaigrette, Fried
Gyoza Skins and Arugula, PAGE 54

71

Potato Crusted Halibut with
Asparagus, Fennel Verjus
and Garlic Mashers, PAGE 58

Ruby Red Trout with Squash,
Mushroom, Chard Ravioli and
Caper Brown Butter, PAGE 60

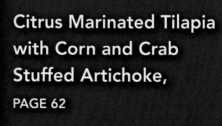

Citrus Marinated Tilapia
with Corn and Crab
Stuffed Artichoke,
PAGE 62

Striped Bass with Summer Squash, Mozzarella and Tomato Tart and Olive Tapanade, PAGE 82

Pecan Crusted Salmon with Apple Sauce and a Smoked Salmon Cake, PAGE 84

Mahi Mahi with Grilled Kale, Udon Noodles and Spicy Peanut Sauce, PAGE 86

Prosciutto Wrapped Monkfish with Chive Gnocchi, Pea and Herb Coulis and Swiss Chard, PAGE 92

Seared Rare Tuna with Crab Fritter, Sriracha Aioli and Vegetable Tempura, PAGE 88

Spice Dusted Scallops with Zucchini Feta Cakes and Yogurt Coulis, PAGE 96

Spicy Glazed Scallops with Mango Salsa, Grilled Kale and Sweet Potato Cakes, PAGE 98

74

Herb Roasted Chicken with Pea Risotto, Haricot Vert and Chicken Jus, PAGE 100

Jerk Chicken with Sweet Potato Mash and Swiss Chard,

PAGE 102

Muscovy Duck Breast with Spinach, Mushrooms, Duck Confit, Pine Nuts and Duck Jus, PAGE 104

75

Seared Elk Short Loin with Asparagus, Vermont Cheddar Potato and Shallot Reduction, PAGE 108

Veal Tenderloin with a Fricassée of Sweetbreads, Artichoke Hearts and Mushrooms with Marsala Reduction, PAGE 114

Petite Filet with Asparagus, Mashers and Barbeque Shrimp, PAGE 116

Herb Crusted Flat Iron Steak with Mushroom-Corn Reduction and Roasted Potatoes, PAGE 118

Flat Iron Steak with Mushrooms,
Haricot Vert, Bleu d'Auvergne Sauce
and Rosemary Roasted Potatoes, PAGE 120

Guinness Braised
Kobe Short Ribs
with Cabbage
and Parsnip
Croquettes,
PAGE 122

Chinese Five Spice
Braised Kobe Short
Ribs with Sweet
Potato Wontons,
PAGE 124

Grilled Pork Chop with
Bacon Cherry Compote
and Braised Cabbage,
PAGE 126

Espresso Ice Cream Cakes
with White Chocolate
Blueberry Crust and
Blueberries, PAGE 132

Molten Chocolate Cake
with Chocolate Chocolate
Chip Ice Cream, Chocolate
Sauce and a Chocolate
Truffle, PAGE 130

Lemon Curd
with Meringue
and Fresh Fruit
and Candied
Jalapeños,
PAGE 134

78

Nutella Crepes with Fresh Fruit and Coconut Ice Cream, PAGE 138

Carrot Cake with Cream Cheese Icing and Candied Carrots, PAGE 136

Chocolate Tart with a Pistachio Crust and Port Poached Cherries, PAGE 142

79

Bruléed Lemon Cheesecake with Fresh Fruit,
PAGE 143

Pecan and Apple Bread Puddings with Vanilla Ice Cream and Caramel Sauce,
PAGE 144

Fruit Beignets, PAGE 146

Striped Bass with Summer Squash, Mozzarella and Tomato Tart & Olive Tapanade

Serves 8

This is a wonderful summer dish. I've enjoyed many a spring and fall eating Nantucket Striped Bass. It is available in June and September and can be hard to catch but everyone has their secret spot. One of my younger cousin's first fish was a keeper Striper. I find that the crisp skin covers a moist and flaky flesh that is quite delectable. I decided to pair it with an Olive Tapanade and give the whole dish a Mediterranean flair. If you can find sun-dried olives, please use them as they are much sweeter than regular brined olives. Use this tomato preparation on salads, in sauces or as a topping for a nice canapé. You may make your own puff pastry but I find frozen to be a nice short cut. The term dock is used here. It is to poke holes into a dough to prevent it from rising.

Summer Squash, Mozzarella and Tomato Tart

10 Roma tomatoes

5 garlic cloves, peeled

5 thyme sprigs

5 basil sprigs

2 cups olive oil

2 sheets puff pastry, defrosted

2 large zucchini

2 large yellow squash

2 large fresh Mozzarella balls

Olive Tapanade

1 cup pitted black olives, sundried or Kalamata

3 tablespoons red pepper, chopped

1 teaspoon ground black pepper

4 anchovy filets, white if possible

1 tablespoon capers, rinsed

Striped Bass

8 6-ounce Striped Bass Filets

½ cup all-purpose flour, in a pie tin or large plate

1 **Summer Squash, Mozzarella and Tomato Tart**: Preheat the oven to 250°. Place 1 gallon of water in a pot over a high heat. Bring the water to a boil. Remove the core from the tomatoes and cut an X into each bottom. Working in batches if necessary, plunge the tomatoes in the boiling water. Allow the tomatoes to cook for about 5 minutes or until the skins begin to flay off. We are not trying to cook the tomatoes but just remove their skins. Transfer the tomatoes to ice water. Cool the tomatoes completely. With a paring knife, scrape the skins from the tomatoes. Quarter the tomatoes lengthwise and remove any seeds. Smash the garlic cloves with the flat side of the knife. Garlic contains allicyn which is the component that provides its pungency. Allycin is not released until the cells of the garlic are broken by smashing or chopping. Place the tomatoes in a roasting pan with the garlic, thyme, basil and olive oil. Roast the tomatoes for 3 hours and cool in a strainer, reserving the oil, garlic and basil.

2 **Preheat the oven to 375°.** Roll the puff pastry to ½-inch thick. Dock the pastry with a fork and cut 8 6-inch diameter circles out of the puff. Place the circles on a parchment lined baking sheet and top with more parchment and a screen or another baking sheet. Bake the circles until cooked, about 10 minutes. Thinly slice the zucchini and yellow squash. Thinly slice mozzarella. Working in a pinwheel, layer zucchini, yellow squash, tomato petals and mozzarella on a puff circle.

3 **Olive Tapanade**: In the food processor, place the garlic cloves and basil leaves from the tomato preparation, as well as the olives, roasted red pepper, black pepper, anchovy filets and capers. Purée the ingredients until they are smooth. With the machine running, add ½ cup of the tomato oil. Reserve the remaining oil for vinaigrettes. Transfer the Olive Tapanade to a squeeze bottle. This will keep, refrigerated for 2 weeks.

4 **Striped Bass**: Preheat oven to 375°. Remove any pin bones or scales from the Striped Bass filets. Score the skin by slicing diagonal shallow cuts into the fish. This is for decoration but also to keep the skin from shriveling up. Heat 2 large pans over high heats. Salt and pepper the fish. Dredge the filets in the flour. Place the filets in the pan, skin side down. Reduce the heat to medium-high. Cook the filets until the skin is crisp, about 5-7 minutes. Flip the fish and cook until the flesh is flaky and white. Keep the fish in a warm area. Place the tarts in the oven. Heat the tarts until they are warm and the cheese has melted, about 10 minutes. Squirt 8 warm plates with Olive Tapanade. Top the Tapanade with a Summer Squash, Mozzarella and Tomato Tart and then with a Striped Bass filet. Serve with a light side salad.

Pecan Crusted Salmon with Apple Sauce & Smoked Salmon Cake

Serves 8

I enjoy this dish because of the Smoked Salmon Cake. We use a hot smoked salmon which has a lot of flavor. I find that the tartness of the Granny Smith apples suits this dish as a contrast to the smoky salmon. If possible use wild salmon, the flavor and the health benefits far surpass farm raised salmon. The Dijon mustard in this recipe works as both a method for adhering the crust as well as a bit of flavor.

Apple Sauce

1 tablespoon olive oil

1 large yellow onion, chopped

4 Granny Smith apples, peeled and chopped

1 heaping tablespoon prepared horseradish

3 cups sake

Smoked Salmon Cakes

¼ cup plus 2 tablespoons yellow cornmeal

3 tablespoons all-purpose flour

¼ teaspoon baking soda

¼ teaspoon Kosher salt

8 ounces hot smoked salmon

1 large egg, beaten lightly

¾ cup buttermilk

2 tablespoons cream cheese, softened

2 tablespoons Chevre

4 tablespoons olive oil

Pecan Crusted Salmon

1 cup pecans

½ cup Parmigiano Reggiano

8 6-ounce portions of salmon, pin bones and skin removed

2 tablespoons olive oil

¼ cup Dijon Mustard

1 **Apple Sauce**: Place a wide pot over a high heat. Add the olive oil to the pot and heat until it shimmers. Add the onion with a pinch of Kosher salt. Reduce the heat to medium-high and stir the onion until it is translucent, about 10 minutes. Add the apple to the pot with a pinch of Kosher salt. Stir the apples into the onion. Cook the apple until it is soft but not mushy, about 10 minutes. Add the horseradish and sake to the pot and bring to a boil. Blend the sauce until it is smooth. If it seems thick, (like well apple sauce) then you may thin it with water. You may keep the sauce in a warm pot or chill it for up to 3 days.

2 **Smoked Salmon Cakes**: Preheat the oven to 350°. In a bowl whisk together cornmeal, flour, baking soda and Kosher salt. Flake the hot smoked salmon into the dry ingredients. Form a well in the center of the dry ingredients. Place the egg, buttermilk, cream cheese and Chevre into the center of the well. Whisk the eggs and gradually combine the wet and dry ingredients. Heat a nonstick pan over a high heat. Add 2 tablespoons olive oil to the pan and heat until it shimmers. Reduce the heat to medium. Too high of a heat will cause the chevre to blacken and burn, so keep your heat on medium. Working in batches add the batter

Pecans

The word pecan is Algonquin for "a nut it takes a stone to crack." These members of the Hicory genus are the fruit of large trees, originating in the Mississippi river valley. The elongated kernel is encased in a smooth, oval, brownish shell. The shell is encased in a fleshy green outer covering that splits easily into four parts when the fruit is ripe. When the hulls covering the pecans burst in the fall, the nuts are ready for harvest. The pecan's flavor improves 3 weeks after harvesting, after which their extremely high fat content makes them an easy target for spoilage. When buying shell-on pecans, choose nuts that are heavy in size and do not rattle when they are shaken. The shells should be unstained and have no cracks or holes.

to the pan using a 2-ounce ice cream scoop. Add as many cakes as the pan will hold but do not crowd the cakes as this slows their cooking. Bubbles should form around the cakes' edges. Cook the cakes until they have brown edges, about 5-6 minutes. Flip the cakes and cook until the other side is crisp, about 5-6 minutes. It's ok if the cakes are a bit underdone in the center as they will continue to cook in the oven. Transfer the cakes to paper towels to remove any excess grease. Wipe the pan clean and add another 2 tablespoons of olive oil to the pan. Once the pan shimmers, begin another batch of cakes. Repeat the process until you have 8 Salmon Corn cakes. Keep the cakes in the warm oven.

3 **Pecan Crusted Salmon**: In a food processor, combine the pecans and Parmigiano Reggiano. Pulse the mixture until it is combined but still coarse. Generously salt and pepper your salmon filets. Salmon has so much

fatty omega 3 oils that the early salting draws some of these oils to the surface and gives the fish a crisp exterior. Place 2 large pans over high heats. Divide the olive oil between the pans and heat until it shimmers. Add the salmon filets to the pan, bone side down. Reduce the heat to medium-high. Cook the salmon filets until they are crisp, about 5 minutes, depending on the thickness of your fish. Whisk the Dijon mustard with 1 tablespoon water. Flip the filets and brush the filet with Dijon mixture. Sprinkle the pecan crust over the fish and place in the oven. Cook the salmon until it is medium, about 5 minutes, depending on the thickness and quality of your fish. The better the quality, the tighter the flesh and slower the cooking process. Divide the warm Smoked Salmon Cakes between 8 hot plates. Top with the Pecan Crusted Salmon and drizzle the Apple Sauce around. A nice wintery salad of Belgian Endive would be a great side dish.

Mahi Mahi with Grilled Kale, Udon Noodles & Spicy Peanut Sauce

Serves 8

Although this book is not presenting any of the items from our vegetarian menu, this is a popular one where we substitute Zucchini for the Mahi Mahi. It is a hearty dish and has been featured in Bon Appetite. Any leftover sauce makes a great chicken glaze or a dipping sauce. You may use any vegetable for this dish but I like the smokiness of grilled kale. Do not salt the kale as the tiniest amount can make the kale super salty.

Spicy Peanut Sauce

½ cup toasted sesame seeds

1 cup peanut butter

5 garlic cloves,
peeled and smashed

¼ cup fresh ginger,
peeled and chopped

½ cup soy

¼ cup rice wine vinegar

2 tablespoons Sriracha
or other Chili Sauce

¼ cup brown sugar

½ cup water

Udon Noodles

20 oz dried udon noodles

Mahi Mahi

2 ½ pounds Mahi Mahi,
skin removed

2 tablespoons olive oil

Grilled Kale

2 bunches green curly kale,
washed and stems removed

1 tablespoon olive oil

½ cup cilantro, roughly chopped

½ cup scallions, finely chopped

1 **Spicy Peanut Sauce**: In a blender, combine all of the ingredients. Blend the ingredients until they are smooth and add more water as needed. Set the peanut sauce aside. It will keep refrigerated for 5 days.

2 **Udon Noodles:** Bring 2 gallons of water to a boil in a large pot. Place the noodles in the boiling water. When the water boils, add one cup of cold water and stir the noodles.

Repeat this process 3 times. After the fourth addition of cold water, turn off the flame and place a lid over the pot. Allow the noodles to steam for 15 minutes. Strain the noodles and rinse with cold water. After rinsing the noodles, place in a pot with enough of the Spicy Peanut Sauce to coat the noodles. Place the pot over a medium heat and constantly stir the noodles. If the sauce gets too thick, thin it with a bit of water.

Kale

The Latin name for kale, *Acephala*, means without a head. This member of the cabbage family received its name because the leaves do not form a head, rather they are attached to fibrous stems. Kale has the ability to withstand harsh weather and temperatures as low as 5 degrees. The younger leaves are sweeter and more tender than the older specimens. When buying, choose kale that is firm and brightly colored with relatively small leaves that are free of spots or mold. Wash the leaves under cool water. If insects are present, swish the leaves in vinegar and water.

Turn the heat to low.

3 **Mahi Mahi**: Heat the grill. Slice the Mahi Mahi into 8 portions. The light brown lines running down the center of the fish may not be attractive but they do not affect the flavor of the fish. Generously salt and pepper the fish. Heat 2 large pans over high heats. Add 1 tablespoon of olive oil to each pan and heat until it shimmers. Add the fish to the pan and cook on one side for 5-6 minutes or until it is slightly crisp around the edges. Flip the fish and cook on the other side until the fish is just cooked through, about 4-5

minutes, depending on the thickness of your fish. Keep the Mahi Mahi warm.

4 **Grilled Kale**: Tear the kale into bite size pieces. Toss the kale in the olive oil. Place the kale on the grill. Using tongs, toss the kale over the hot coals until it is wilted. Place the Udon Noodles over a medium high heat and stir frequently. When the noodles are hot, add the cilantro and scallions and stir to combine. Divide the hot noodles between the 8 hot bowls. Top the noodles with the Grilled Kale and then the Mahi Mahi . Serve to hungry guests.

Seared Rare Tuna with Crab Fritter, Sriracha Aioli & Vegetable Tempura

Serves 8

Hawaiian Ahi Tuna is one of the more delicious delicacies of the world. When fresh and properly caught, tuna can be as soft as butter and melt in your mouth. I am lucky to use Honolulu Fish that will Federal Express me fresh Tuna in 36 hours. It is a shame to serve this fish anything but rare. This recipe shows you 2 ways to make a mayonnaise, by mixer or blender. You may also whisk in the oil by hand, if you have the time and gumption. You will have a few extra Crab Fritters but they make a great snack for a hungry chef. Here, I use Sweet Potato and Zucchini Tempura but you may use whatever strikes your fancy.

Sriracha Aioli

80 grams of pasteurized egg yolks or 4 fresh yolks

½ cup olive oil

¼ cup Sriracha or other Hot Chili Sauce

Crab Fritter

80 grams of pasteurized egg yolks or 4 fresh yolks

½ cup olive oil

2 teaspoons Old Bay Seasoning

2 tablespoons parsley leaves, chopped

2 tablespoons scallions, finely chopped

1 pound back fin crabmeat

1 pound jumbo lump crabmeat

2 cups panko breadcrumbs

Vegetable Tempura

3 extra large eggs

1 cup cornstarch

1 tablespoon sesame oil

4 cups all-purpose flour

4 cups cold water

1 quart canola oil

2 medium sweet potatoes, peeled and cut into large match sticks

2 large zucchini, sliced thickly

Seared Rare Ahi Tuna

2 pounds Ahi tuna, any sinew blood line or skin removed

2 tablespoons olive oil

1 **Sriracha Aioli**: Place the egg yolks in the bowl of a standing mixer. Start mixing the yolks at a high speed. When the yolks thicken slightly, reduce the speed to medium-high and slowly drizzle in ¼ cup of olive oil. Add the Sriracha and continue to mix. Slowly add the remaining olive oil. The mixture should be thick. Transfer the aioli to a squeeze bottle and chill. This will keep refrigerated for 2 weeks.

2 **Crab Fritter**: In a blender, place the egg yolks. Start mixing the yolks at a high speed. When the yolks thicken slightly, reduce the speed to medium-high and slowly drizzle in ¼ cup of olive oil. Add the Old Bay, parsley and scallions and blend until combined. Slowly drizzle in the remaining olive oil and transfer the mixture to a bowl. Add the 2 crabmeats to the bowl and mix thoroughly but try to preserve the lumps. Place the panko in a shallow bowl or pie tin. Portion the crab fritters, using a 2 ounce ice cream scoop. Squeeze any excess water out of the crab fritters and roll them in the panko. Chill the fritters for 30 minutes.

3 **Vegetable Tempura**: Preheat the oven to 300°. Whisk together the eggs, cornstarch, sesame oil, flour and water. Set the tempura batter aside. Place the oil in a pot over a high heat. Once the oil is hot, reduce the heat to medium. You may test the oil by adding a cube of bread. If the cube browns, your oil is hot. Working in batches, dip the sweet potato and zucchini in the tempura batter and fry until golden, about 7 minutes for the sweet potato and 5 minutes for the zucchini. Transfer the vegetables to paper towels, lightly salt and

keep warm in the oven. Increase the canola oil's heat to medium-high. Working in batches, fry the Crab Fritters until golden and warm in the center. Lightly salt the Crab Fritters and keep them warm in the oven

4 **Seared Rare Ahi Tuna**: Slice the tuna into 8 portions. Kosher salt and pepper the portions. Place 2 large pans over high heats. Divide the olive oil between the 2 pans and heat until it shimmers. Add the tuna portions to the pans and sear on all sides, about 5-7 minutes. Sear the tuna so the outside edges are crisp and the center is still bright red and a bit cool. Slice the Seared Rare Tuna and divide between 8 warmed plates. Top with the Vegetable Tempura and a Crab Fritter. Squirt the plates with the Sriracha Aioli and serve.

Seared Rare Hebi with Tomato & Garlic Steamed Clams, Asparagus & Mushroom Polenta

Serves 8

I just learned of Hebi this year and I love it. It is in the Marlin family and is among the smaller Marlin. Seared rare it is giving our Ahi Tuna dish a run for its money. We get the Hebi and Tuna delivered directly from Hawaii and the quality is always fabulous. This dish travels away from the usual Asian flavors you'd find with a seared rare fish and goes for some old fashioned tomato and basil steamed clams. The result is a flavorful and warming dish.

Hebi can be expensive but the filling clams allow you to serve a smaller portion. The polenta is a recipe that differs with the conditions. Depending on the fat content of the butter and the weather, your polenta may be a bit soft. If the butter has a high water content and low fat content that will add excess liquid to the polenta. If it is a humid day, the polenta may need less liquid. The older a clam is the more easily they'll open when cooked. As with all live shellfish, discard any that have cracks or holes before cooking and any that do not open after cooking.

Mushroom Polenta

1 cup crimini mushrooms, stems removed

1 cup shiitake mushrooms, stems removed

1 cup oyster mushrooms, stems removed

2 tablespoons olive oil

6 cups chicken stock

2 cups yellow cornmeal

1/3 cup heavy whipping cream

2 tablespoons unsalted butter

1 cup Parmigiano Reggiano, grated finely

1/4 cup fresh oregano, chopped

3 cups canola oil

Tomato & Garlic Steamed Clams

2 tablespoons unsalted butter

2 pounds Manila or other small clams

1 cup white wine

1 1/2 cups tomatoes, peeled, seeded and chopped

1 tablespoon garlic, chopped

1/4 cup chopped basil

8 5-ounce portions of Hebi, skin removed

2 tablespoons olive oil

1 bunch asparagus

1 **Mushroom Polenta**: Chop the mushrooms and keep them separate. Place a large pan over a high heat. Add 1 tablespoon of olive oil and heat until it shimmers. Reduce the heat to medium. Add the crimini mushrooms to the pan with a pinch of Kosher salt. Stir the mushrooms for about 2 minutes or until they just begin to release their water. Add the shiitake mushrooms to the pan with a pinch of Kosher salt. Stir the mushrooms until they begin to release their water. Add the oyster mushrooms. Cook the mushrooms until they release all of their water and brown on the edges, about 5 minutes. Cool the mushrooms.

2 **Place the chicken stock in a large pot** over a high heat and bring to a boil. Whisk the cornmeal into the boiling water and reduce the heat to medium. Continue to whisk until the mixture is smooth with no lumps, about 15-20 minutes. Add the cream and butter. Continue to stir until the butter has melted. Take the polenta off of the heat and add the Parmigiano Reggiano, oregano and mushrooms. Oil a baking sheet with the remaining olive oil. Spread the polenta onto the baking sheet and chill until cool, about 5 hours.

3 **Asparagus**: Place 2 quarts of water with 2 tablespoons Kosher salt over a high heat and bring the water to a rapid boil. When working with asparagus, I like to break off the ends as opposed to cutting them off. This ensures you're discarding most of the tough fibers. That said, break the tough ends off of the asparagus. Plunge the asparagus into the boiling water and allow to cook for 7-8 minutes or until the spears are tender. Transfer the asparagus to a bowl of ice water and cool completely. Drain the ice water off of the asparagus and chop the spears into bite size pieces.

4 **When the polenta is cool**, slice it into triangles. Preheat the oven to 275°. Place the canola oil in a pot over a high heat. When the oil is hot, reduce the heat to medium-high. Working in batches, fry the triangles until they are crisp. If your polenta is a bit soft, dredge it in a little flour before frying. Transfer the polenta to paper towels, removing any excess grease. Fry 16 triangles and keep them warm in the oven.

5 **Tomato and Garlic Steamed Clams**: Place in a pot, the butter, clams, white wine, tomatoes and garlic. Place a lid over the pot and place the pot over a high heat. Allow the clams to steam until they open, about 10-15 minutes depending on the age of your clams. While the clams are steaming, generously salt and pepper the Hebi filets. Heat 2 large pans over high heats. Divide the olive oil between the 2 pans and heat until it shimmers. Add the filets to the pan and brown on all sides, about 5 minutes depending on the thickness of your fish. Transfer the Hebi to a cutting board. Add the chopped asparagus to the clam pot and heat through. Add the basil to the Tomato and Garlic Steamed Clams and toss to combine. Divide the clams and broth between 8 warm bowls. Slice the Hebi filets and place on top of the clams. Place the Mushroom Polenta on the sides and serve.

Prosciutto Wrapped Monkfish with Chive Gnocchi, Pea and Herb Coulis & Swiss Chard

Serves 8

Few fish stand up to the intense flavor of Prosciutto but Monkfish was made for it. Monkfish has a firm texture and a sweet flavor. This firm texture gave it the nickname, poor man's lobster. In recent years, many have discovered what a lovely fish this is and the price has risen considerably. It is an ugly fish, whose tail yields the only edible meat. You may not use a masher for the potato gnocchi. The ricer is imperative as it produces a smooth potato product. The gnocchi recipe is time consuming, so blanch the chard while making the gnocchi. If the prosciutto is not thin, it won't adhere to the fish properly. The ham is salty enough so season the Monkfish with pepper only. You may cook the Monkfish on the stove top solely but the oven will crisp up the ham as well as cook the fish.

Pea and Herb Coulis

1 tablespoon olive oil

1 large onion, chopped

1 leek, white and green parts only, cleaned of any dirt and chopped

2 garlic cloves, peeled and chopped

2 cups chicken stock

1 cup heavy whipping cream

½ cup parsley leaves

½ cup basil leaves

¼ cup chives

¼ cup oregano leaves

2 cups peas, frozen are fine but the blanching time will be less

Chive Gnocchi

3 pounds Yukon Gold potatoes, peeled and thinly sliced

11 ounces all-purpose flour

3 egg yolks

¼ cup chives, finely chopped

2 tablespoons olive oil

2 tablespoons unsalted butter, melted

Swiss Chard

2 bunches Swiss chard, trimmed

¼ cup chicken stock

2 tablespoons butter

Prosciutto Wrapped Monkfish

2 pounds Monkfish filet, cleaned of any membrane

16 thin prosciutto slices

2 tablespoons olive oil

1 **Pea and Herb Coulis**: Place 2 quarts of water with 2 tablespoons of Kosher salt over a high heat. Place a wide pot over a high heat. When the pan is hot add the olive oil. Add the onion with a pinch of Kosher salt and reduce the heat to medium-high. Stirring the onion frequently, cook it until it has brown edges, about 10 minutes. Add the leek and garlic to the pot and cook until they are translucent, about 5 minutes. Add the chicken stock to the pan and increase the heat to high. Reduce the stock by half and add the cream. Reduce the cream by half and set the mixture aside. Plunge the parsley, basil, chives and oregano in the boiling water and blanch until they are bright green, about 3 minutes. Transfer the herbs to an ice bath and cool completely. Drain any water off of the herbs and squeeze out any excess water. Plunge the peas into the water and blanch them until they are bright green and floating to the surface, about 5 minutes. Transfer the peas to an ice bath and cool completely. Drain the water off of the peas. Working in batches, blend the cream mixture, herbs and peas until smooth. Set the Pea and Herb Coulis aside. This will keep for 1 week refrigerated.

2 **Chive Gnocchi**: Place the potatoes in a pot and cover with cold water. Add a pinch of Kosher salt to the potatoes and place over a high heat. When the water comes to a boil, reduce the heat to medium and simmer the potatoes until they are tender, about 45 minutes to an hour. Strain the potatoes and run them through a food mill. Cool the potatoes completely. Place 2 quarts of water in a pot over a high heat. In a bowl, combine 33 ounces of the cooled potato with the flour, egg yolks, chives and as much salt and pepper as you like. Roll the mixture into a long snake and slice into ½ inch pieces. When the water comes to a boil, add half of the gnocchi to the boiling water. Allow the gnocchi to rise to the surface and then cook for 3 minutes. Transfer the gnocchi to a tray. Repeat with the remaining gnocchi and refrigerate them until they are cool. Heat a large skillet over a high heat, add half of the olive oil to the pan and heat until it shimmers. Add half of the butter to the pan and reduce the heat to medium high. When the butter stops foaming, add half of the gnocchi. Do not move the gnocchi but allow them to brown for 3 minutes. When 1 side is crisp, flip the gnocchi with a spatula and brown on the other side, about 4-5 minutes. Transfer the gnocchi to a baking tray. Wipe the pan clean and repeat the process with the remaining gnocchi. Set the gnocchi in a warm area, on a baking sheet.

3 **Swiss Chard**: Place 2 quarts of water with 2 tablespoons of Kosher salt over a high heat. Plunge the chard leaves into the boiling water and allow to cook for 7-8 minutes or until the leaves are tender. Transfer the chard to a bowl of ice water and cool completely. Drain any water off of the chard and place in a pot with the remaining butter, chicken stock and salt and pepper, to your liking.

4 **Prosciutto Wrapped Monkfish**: Preheat the oven to 400°. Slice the monkfish into 8 portions. Lay 2 prosciutto slices side by side, overlapping slightly, on a flat surface. Place a Monkfish portion on 1 end of the slices. Roll the prosciutto around the Monkfish, forming a tight cylinder. Repeat with the remaining prosciutto and Monkfish. If not using straight away, chill the Monkfish. Slice each portion of the Prosciutto Wrapped Monkfish into 3 or 4 medallions. Place 2 large pans over a high heat. Divide the olive oil between the 2 pans and heat until it shimmers. Divide the medallions between the pans and reduce the heat to medium-high. Cook the Monkfish until it is brown and crisp, about 5 minutes. Flip the Prosciutto Wrapped Monkfish and place it in the oven until it is cooked through, about 7-9 minutes.

5 **Reheat the Chive Gnocchi in the oven** for about 5 minutes or until they are hot. Place the Pea and Herb Coulis in a pot over a medium high heat. Whisk the Coulis frequently until it is hot. Place the Swiss Chard over a high heat and cook until it is steaming hot. Drizzle a bit of Pea and Herb Coulis onto 8 warm plates. Place the Swiss Chard in the center of the plates and place the Prosciutto Wrapped Monkfish on the plates. Add the Chive Gnocchi and serve.

Sesame & Panko Crusted Softshell Crabs with Rice Noodles & Coconut Milk Reduction

Serves 8

Growing up in Virginia, I often saw Softshell Crabs on restaurant menus. My mother would always order them and I grew to love eating off of her plate. I always loved crabmeat but softshell crabs gave crab a new meaning. The crisp skin covers the firm crab flesh that explodes in the mouth with a sweet and salty sensation. The softshell crab business is usually a family run show. If a crab has a pink mark on its back fin, it will molt within the week. This crab is taken to a tank and observed until it sheds its outer shell. It is then plucked from the tank and sent all over the country, still alive. My favorite preparation is a pair of sautéed softshell crabs, asparagus and a side of lemon wedges. Use a fine strainer for the Coconut Milk Reduction, so all of the lemongrass is extracted.

Coconut Milk Reduction

1 tablespoon olive oil

4 cups shrimp shells

2 whole bay leaves

1 can coconut milk

1 stalk lemongrass

Rice Noodles

1 package dried rice noodles

2 large or 3 small zucchini, finely sliced

1 large red pepper, seeds and core removed and finely sliced

1 carrot, sliced into fine matchsticks

3 tablespoons black sesame seeds

3 tablespoons unsalted butter

Sesame and Panko Crusted Softshell Crabs

½ cup panko breadcrumbs

½ cup toasted white sesame seeds

½ cup Parmigiano Reggiano, grated

16 jumbo or larger softshell crabs

4 tablespoons olive oil

1 cup all-purpose flour

½ cup chopped fresh basil

1 **Coconut Milk Reduction**: Place a pot over a high heat. Add the olive oil and heat until it shimmers, about 1 minute. Reduce the heat to medium-high and add the shrimp shells with a pinch of Kosher salt and the bay leaves. Stir the shells until they are just turning pink. Add enough cold water to just cover the shells. When the water comes to a boil, reduce the heat to medium and simmer the shells for 25 minutes. Strain the shells through a fine mesh strainer. Place 2 cups of the strained liquid in a blender with the can of coconut milk. With a meat tenderizer, pound the lemongrass until it breaks apart. Remove the greener, reedy end and place the lighter flesh in the blender. Blend the ingredients until they are smooth. Set the mixture aside. You may use any remaining shrimp stock or fumet to flavor a nice soup or sauce.

Sesame Seeds

These highly nutritious seeds are extremely perishable, so freeze any surplus. Their oil represents over half of their total weight. They take on a sweet, nutty flavor when roasted so by all means, pop them in the oven. They are an excellent source of magnesium, potassium, iron, calcium, phosphorus, zinc, copper, thiamine, niacin, folic acid and vitamin B6. They are a rich source of dietary fiber and contain riboflavin. They act as an antiarthritic, emollient and laxative. Sesame seeds are beneficial for the nervous system, aid digestion and activate blood circulation. Before you down a handful of seeds, know that the nutrients are better assimilated in an oil, paste or butter form.

2 **Rice Noodles**: Cover the rice noodles with boiling hot water. Allow the noodles to steep until they are soft, about 10-15 minutes. Combine the zucchini, red pepper, carrot and black sesame seeds in a large pot with the butter. Strain the water off of the rice noodles and add to the pot. Strain the coconut milk mixture into the pot and set the pot aside.

3 **Sesame and Panko Crusted Softshell Crabs**: Preheat the oven to 400°. In a bowl, combine the panko, sesame seed and Parmigiano Reggiano. Tear the back flap or apron off of the crabs. They should still be squirming. Remove the eyes and the water sac that lies behind the eyes. If this is left in, it will pop grease on you during cooking. Lift up both of the side flaps and remove the finger-like gills. Place 2 large pans over high heats. Kosher salt and pepper the crabs and dredge them in the flour. Divide the olive oil between the pans and heat the oil until it shimmers. Add the crabs, pink side down and reduce the heat to medium. Sauté the crabs until they are crisp, about 7-10 minutes. Flip the crabs and sprinkle the panko mixture over the tops. Place the pans in the oven to finish the cooking, about 5-7 minutes. Place the Rice Noodle pot over a high heat. Once the noodles begin steaming, stir in the basil. Divide the noodles and broth between 8 warmed bowls. Lift a flap of 1 of the crabs and ensure the meat is white and firm. Place 2 crabs on top of the noodles in each bowl and serve.

Spice Dusted Scallops with Zucchini Feta Cakes & Yogurt Coulis

Serves 8

This is a slightly newer Scallop dish that I wanted to serve for a long time. I was nervous that my guests would miss the Scallop dish that I had been serving for years, the one following this one. I was wrong. I've received nothing but compliments on this dish. The flavors are reminiscent of Moroccan Cuisine. Feel free to fry up the Zucchini Feta cakes ahead of time and reheat them in the oven. Make sure you're using the larger Sea Scallops and not small Bay Scallops. I remember that Bay Scallops are the small variety because bay and baby sound alike.

Yogurt Coulis

2 cucumbers, peeled and seeded

1 ½ cups yogurt

½ cup sour cream

juice of 1 lime

¼ cup fresh oregano leaves

¼ cup roasted red pepper

Spice Dust

3 tablespoons whole mustard seed

3 tablespoons whole cumin seed

3 tablespoons whole coriander seed

3 tablespoons white sesame seed

½ cup panko breadcrumbs

Zucchini Feta Cakes

5 cups grated zucchini

2 teaspoons Kosher salt

2 eggs

2 yolks

1 cup all-purpose flour

1 cup Feta cheese, drained of excess juice

1 cup parsley, chopped

½ cup finely chopped scallions

6 tablespoons olive oil

3 pounds or 24 large Sea Scallops, tough side-muscle removed

2 tablespoons olive oil

1 **Yogurt Coulis:** Place in a blender the cucumbers, yogurt, sour cream, lime juice, oregano leaves and roasted red pepper. Blend the ingredients until smooth and transfer to a squeeze bottle. This sauce is better made a day ahead to allow the flavors to marry. It will keep for 5 days refrigerated.

2 **Spice Dust:** Preheat the oven to 400°. Place the mustard seed, cumin seed, coriander seed and sesame seed on a baking sheet. Place the spices in the oven and allow to roast for 5 minutes or until they are fragrant. Cool the seeds slightly and grind in a spice grinder or small coffee grinder. Grind the spices until they are fine. Transfer the spices to a bowl with the panko. Rub the panko and spices between your hands, breaking up the panko in the process. Set the spice dust aside.

3 **Zucchini Feta Cakes**: Toss the zucchini in the Kosher salt and allow to stand in a colander for 15 minutes. Squeeze as much liquid as possible out of the zucchini. Place the zucchini in a bowl and add the eggs, yolks, flour, Feta, parsley and scallions. Mix thoroughly. Heat a non-stick pan over a high heat. Place 2 tablespoons of olive oil in the pan. Once the oil begins to shimmer, reduce the heat to medium. Working in batches, scoop sand dollar sized patties into the pan. Brown on one side until they are crisp, about 4-6 minutes. Flip the cakes and brown the other side until crisp, about 5-7 minutes. Transfer the cakes to paper towels, removing any excess grease. Make 16 cakes. The batter will keep for 3 days, refrigerated.

4 **Preheat the oven to 350°.** Salt and pepper the scallops. Drag 1 flat side of a scallop through the Spice Dust. Repeat with the remaining scallops. Heat 2 large pans over high heats. Divide the olive oil between the 2 pans and heat until it shimmers. Reduce the heat to medium and add the scallops, crust side down. Allow the scallops to sear for about 3 minutes. Flip the scallops and sear on the other side until just cooked through. Depending on the size of your scallop, about 4-5 minutes. Reheat the cakes in the oven for 10 minutes. Divide the hot Zucchini Feta Cakes between 8 warm plates. Drizzle the Yogurt Coulis around and place the Spice Dusted Scallops on top. You may opt for a side salad as well but the flavor of the zucchini cakes provides ample vegetal flavor.

Spicy Glazed Scallops with Mango Salsa, Grilled Kale & Sweet Potato Cakes

Serves 8

I am lucky enough to have a father that loves to sail in the Carribean. We spent many a Christmas and Spring Break listening to steel drums and drinking Red Stripe. The flavors of the islands emerge in some of my dishes and this is one. The spice of the glaze, the sweet of the mango and the earthy flavor of the sweet potato cakes work together for a balanced dish with a punch of spice. The slightly darker flap that is on the side of a scallop, is the abductor muscle that allows the scallop to swim. It is very tough and should be removed and discarded. It should be noted that the scallop is a strong swimmer and the only migratory bivalve.

Spicy Glaze

1 ripe mango, peeled

¼ cup Sriracha hot sauce

2 cups sugar

1 tablespoon lemon juice

½ cup water

Sweet Potato Cakes

4 large or 5 small sweet potatoes

1 ½ cups Parmigiano Reggiano, grated

2 tablespoons rosemary, chopped

2 cups panko breadcrumbs

2 cups canola oil

1 cup all-purpose flour

4 eggs, beaten

Mango Salsa

3 ripe mangoes, peeled

juice of 1 lime

3 tablespoons roasted red pepper, finely chopped

2 tablespoons scallions, finely chopped

2 tablespoons flat leaf parsley, chopped

Grilled Kale

3 tablespoons olive oil

2 bunches kale, stems removed and rinsed of any dirt

3 pounds or 24 large Sea Scallops, tough side-muscle removed

1 **Spicy Glaze:** Cut the flesh of the mango off of the flat center pit and place in a blender with the Sriracha. Place the sugar, lemon juice and water in a pot over a high heat. Bring the mixture to a boil. Keeping a close eye, boil until the mixture thickens and turns an amber color, about 10 minutes. Remove the sugar from the heat. Carefully add the sugar to the blender and blend until smooth. Transfer the spicy glaze to a squeeze bottle and chill. This will keep for a month refrigerated.

Mango

The mango is a relative of the pistachio and cashew. The mango tree is a handsome evergreen with a smooth, grey trunk and a spreading canopy of dark green foliage. The fruits hang from the boughs on short ropes like Christmas ornaments. These tropical trees enjoy wet and warm climates and grow to a height of 50-100 feet. They have an annual yield of 100 fruits. There exist over 1000 different varieties of mango whose shapes range from oval to kidney. Mangoes are an average of 4 inches long and weigh anywhere from 9 ounces to 3 pounds. Within the smooth inedible skin, the flesh is orange or peach colored. Choose unbruised fruit with a soft yet firm flesh. Test for ripeness by cradling in the palm of your hand and giving a gentle squeeze. Ripe fruit will yield slightly. Avoid very soft fruit, those with black spots as well as green or rock hard mangoes. They will ripen at room temperature or faster in a paper bag. Ripe mangoes will keep refrigerated for 1-2 weeks.

2 **Sweet Potato Cakes**: Preheat the oven to 400°. Rinse the sweet potatoes and prick the skins with a fork. Place the sweet potatoes on a baking sheet. Place the baking sheet in the oven and roast for about 45 minutes or until they are soft. Cool the sweet potatoes. Once they are cool enough to handle, remove the skins and add the Parmigiano Reggiano, rosemary and 1 cup of the panko. Mix thoroughly and chill for 1 hour. Preheat the oven to 300°. Form the sweet potato mixture into small cakes. Place the flour, egg and remaining panko in separate shallow bowls or pie tins. Dredge the cakes in the flour, then the egg, then the panko. Heat the canola oil over a high heat. Once the oil begins to shimmer, reduce the heat to medium. Working in batches, fry the cakes until they are crisp. Transfer the cakes to paper towels to remove any excess grease. Lightly salt the cakes and place them in the oven to keep warm.

3 **Mango Salsa**: Remove the pit and dice the flesh of the mangoes. In a bowl, combine the mangoes, lime juice, red pepper, scallions and parsley. Set aside and allow the flavors to marry.

4 **Grilled Kale**: Light the grill. Heat 2 large pans over high heats. Lightly salt and pepper the scallops. Heat 1 tablespoon of the olive oil in each pan, until it shimmers. Working in batches, sear the scallops until all sides are crisp, about 5-7 minutes, depending on the size of your scallops. While the scallops are searing, toss the kale in the remaining oil. Place the kale on the hot grill. With tongs, move the kale around the grill until it is wilted. Divide the kale among 8 warmed plates. Place 2 cakes on each plate and a bit of the salsa in the middle. Squirt a bit of spicy glaze onto the scallops and divide among the 8 plates. Serve to hungry guests.

Herb Roasted Chicken with Pea Risotto, Haricot Vert & Chicken Jus

Serves 8

We change the herbs in this chicken dish to suit my fancy. In the spring we'll have tarragon and lemon. In the winter, sage and orange. The herbs that make the most people happy are rosemary and parsley. So please use this herb butter as a starting point and then go wild with fresh herbs, chives, basil, sorrel etc. You will have some Herb Butter left over but it brightens up any vegetable dish. The peas will cook in the risotto. If they are fresh, they will lend a lovely crunchiness to the dish.

Chicken Jus

4 whole 4-pound chickens

¼ cup juniper berries, crushed

5 oregano sprigs

2 cups tomatoes, peeled, seeded and chopped

2 quarts veal stock

Herb Butter

1 pound unsalted butter

sections of 1 lemon, no seeds or pith

sections of 1 orange, no seeds or pith

1 tablespoon sage, chopped

1 tablespoon, parsley, chopped

1 tablespoon rosemary, chopped

Pea Risotto

6 cups chicken stock

1 tablespoon olive oil

1 small yellow onion, finely chopped

2 cups peas, fresh or frozen

2 cups risotto, Arborio or Carnoli

½ cup Parmigiano Reggiano, grated

2 tablespoons unsalted butter

¼ cup parsley, chopped

2 tablespoons olive oil

Haricot Vert

1 pound haricot vert, trimmed

2 tablespoons unsalted butter

½ cup chicken stock

1 **Chicken Jus**: Preheat the oven to 400°. Using a very sharp knife, separate the breasts and legs from the chicken carcass. Leave the skin of the breasts intact and reserve the legs for another use. With a cleaver, chop the top end of the drummette bone off of the chicken breast. Leave the rest of the bone in for decoration. Repeat this process with the remaining chickens. Chill the breasts until ready to use. Remove any liver, lungs or kidneys from the carcasses. With a cleaver, chop the carcasses and necks into 2-inch pieces. Place the chicken pieces in a wide, oven safe pot. Add the juniper berries and a dash of salt. Place the bones in the oven and roast until the bones are dark brown, about 45 minutes. Place the pot over a medium-high heat. Add the oregano sprigs and tomatoes. Stir the bones to release any bits of protein on the pan's bottom. Add the veal stock and bring to a boil. Reduce the heat to medium and simmer for 2 hours. Strain the Chicken Jus, through a fine strainer into another pot over a medium-high heat. Reduce the Chicken Jus by half. Chill the Chicken Jus until ready to use.

2 **Herb Butter**: Place in a food processor, the lemon sections, orange sections, sage, parsley and rosemary. Blend the ingredients until smooth and then add the butter in chunks. Once the mixture is fully combined, spread onto a tray and chill.

3 **Pea Risotto**: Place the chicken stock in a pot over a high heat. When the stock comes to a boil, reduce the heat to medium-low. Place a wide pot over a high heat. Add the olive oil to the pot and heat until it shimmers. Add the chopped onion and reduce the heat to medium. Add a dash of salt and stir the onions. Sweat the onions for 7 minutes or until they are translucent without any color. Rinse the risotto and add it to the pot. Stir the risotto into the onions until the rice is shiny. Ladle approximately a quarter of the hot chicken stock into the risotto. Stir until the risotto has absorbed all of the stock. Ladle half of the remaining stock into the risotto and stir until the risotto has absorbed all of the stock. Add the remaining stock into the risotto and stir until all of the stock has been absorbed. Add the peas and set the risotto aside.

4 **Haricot Vert**: Place a pot with 2 quarts of cold water and 2 tablespoons Kosher salt over a high heat. We start with cold water because there are minerals that crystalize in your hot water pipes and they can discolor your food and give it an off flavor. If you prefer to add your salt when the water is already at a boil, be careful as this causes a severe bubbling reaction. When the water comes to a boil, add the haricot vert and allow to cook for 5 minutes or until they are a bright green but with a bit of crunch. Transfer the haricot vert to an ice bath and chill until completely cool. Drain off the ice water and place the haricot vert in a pot with the butter, chicken stock and salt and pepper to your liking.

5 **Preheat the oven to 400°**. Stuff enough butter under the skin of the chickens to cover the entire length and width of the skin. Kosher salt and pepper the chickens. Place 2 large pans over high heats. Add 1 tablespoon of olive oil to each of the pans. Once the oil is hot, place the chickens into the pans, skin side down. Reduce the heat to medium. Sear the chicken breasts on the skin side for 5-7 minutes or until the skin is browned. Quite a bit of butter will ooze out so be careful of the popping grease. Turn the chickens onto the flesh side and place in the oven for 10-15 minutes or until they are cooked through. Allow the chickens to rest in a warm area for 5 minutes. Place the Haricot Vert over a medium-high heat and heat until it is steaming. Place the Pea Risotto over a medium-high heat. Stirring constantly slowly reheat the Pea Risotto for 5 minutes, or until it is hot. Add the Parmigiano Reggiano, butter and parsley and stir until it is a warm and creamy delight. Bring the Chicken Jus to a boil. Slice the Herb Roasted Chicken. Divide the Pea Risotto among 8 warmed plates and top with the Haricot Vert. Top the Pea Risotto with the Herb Roasted Chicken and drizzle the Chicken Jus around.

Jerk Chicken with Sweet Potato Mash & Swiss Chard

Serves 8

I have spent a lot of time sailing in the Carribean and Jerk spices hold a special place in my heart. This dish travels away from the Classic French you usually see in my dishes to a more vibrant flavor. This recipe makes quite a bit of butter. Put pats on warm rice cakes or vegetables that need a little kick.

Chicken Jus

4 whole 4-pound chickens

¼ cup juniper berries, crushed

5 thyme sprigs

2 cups tomatoes, peeled, seeded and chopped

2 quarts veal stock

Jerk Butter

3 scallions, chopped

4 garlic cloves, smashed

¼ cup chopped yellow onion

3 dried chili d'arbols
or other dried chili

2 tablespoons lime juice

2 tablespoons soy sauce

1 tablespoon Kosher salt

1 tablespoon brown sugar

1 tablespoon thyme leaves

2 teaspoons allspice

2 teaspoons black pepper, finely ground

¾ teaspoon nutmeg, ground

½ teaspoon cinnamon, fresh ground

1 pound unsalted butter

Sweet Potato Mash

5 small or 4 large
sweet potatoes

3 tablespoons brown sugar

2 tablespoons tamarind paste, soaked in warm water and seeds removed

2 tablespoons unsalted butter

Swiss Chard

2 bunches red Swiss chard

2 tablespoons unsalted butter

¼ cup chicken stock

2 tablespoons olive oil

1 **Chicken Jus**: Preheat the oven to 400°. Using a very sharp knife, separate the breasts and legs from the chicken carcass. Leave the skin of the breasts intact and reserve the legs for another use. With a cleaver, chop the top end of the drummette bone off of the chicken breast. Leave the rest of the bone in for decoration. Repeat with the remaining chickens. Chill the breasts until ready to use. Remove any liver, lungs or kidneys from the carcasses. With a cleaver, chop the carcasses and necks into 2 inch pieces. Place the chicken pieces in a wide, oven safe pot. Add the juniper berries and a dash of Kosher salt. Place the bones in the oven and roast until the bones are dark brown, about 45 minutes. Place the pot over a medium-high heat. Add the thyme sprigs and tomatoes. Stir the bones to release any bits of protein from the pan's bottom. Add the veal stock and bring to a boil. Reduce the heat to medium and simmer for 2 hours. Strain the Chicken Jus, through a fine strainer into another pot over a medium-high heat. Reduce the Chicken Jus by half. Set the Jus aside or refrigerate it.

2 **Jerk Butter**: Place in a food processor, the scallions, garlic cloves, onion, chili d'arbols, lime juice, soy sauce, Kosher salt, brown sugar, thyme leaves, allspice, pepper, nutmeg and cinnamon. Blend the ingredients until smooth and then add the 1 pound of butter in chunks. Once the mixture is fully combined, spread onto a tray and chill.

3 **Sweet Potato Mash**: Preheat the oven to 400°. Wash the sweet potatoes and prick all over with a fork. Place the sweet potatoes in the oven and roast for 45 minutes to 1 hour or until they are soft. Remove the skins from the sweet potatoes and place the flesh into a pot with the brown sugar, tamarind paste and butter. Set the pot aside.

4 **Swiss Chard**: Bring 2 quarts of water to a boil with 2 tablespoons of Kosher salt. Trim any stem off of the chard leaves. Plunge the leaves into the boiling water and allow to cook for 7-8 minutes or until the leaves are tender. Transfer the chard to a bowl of ice water and cool completely. Drain any water off of the chard and place in a pot with the butter, chicken stock and a bit of salt and pepper.

5 **Preheat the oven to 400°.** Stuff enough butter under the skin of the chickens, to cover the entire length and width of the skin. Salt and pepper the chickens. Place 2 large pans over high heats. When the pans are hot, add 1 tablespoon olive oil to each pan. When the oil is hot, place the chickens into the pans, skin side down. Reduce the heat to medium. Sear the chicken breasts on the skin side for 5-7 minutes or until the skin is browned. Quite a bit of butter will ooze out so be careful of the popping grease. Turn the chickens onto the flesh side and place in the oven for 10-12 minutes or until they are cooked through. Allow the chickens to rest in a warm area for 5 minutes.

6 **Place the pot of sweet potatoes** over a medium-high heat and stir occasionally until warm. Heat the Swiss Chard over a medium-high heat until steaming. Bring the Chicken Jus to a boil. Divide the Sweet Potato Mash between 8 warmed plates and top with the Swiss Chard. Slice the Jerk Chicken and place on top of the Swiss Chard. Drizzle the hot Chicken Jus around the plate and serve.

Muscovy Duck Breast with Spinach, Mushrooms, Duck Confit, Pine Nuts & Duck Jus

Serves 8

I love duck and this dish allows the duck to shine in three different ways. At 221, we first butcher the duck and make the bones into a stock with mushroom stems. The stock is then reduced with port, making a Duck Jus. We toss the legs in a dry cure and weight them for 48 hours. The legs are then cooked slowly in their own fat for three and a half hours, making Duck Confit. Finally, we sear the breast slowly to crisp the skin but keep the meat juicy. All of these components produce a beautiful dish. You may have some leftover Duck Confit. It's great in stews or as a topping for a simple salad with Chevre. This recipe takes a few days, so plan ahead.

Duck Jus

4 whole Muscovy Hens

4 cups shiitake mushrooms, stems removed and reserved.

2 cups port

Duck Confit

½ cup sugar

½ cup Kosher salt

3 tablespoons chopped garlic

½ cup pine nuts

5 tablespoons olive oil

1 tablespoon unsalted butter

4 cups fresh spinach, picked of any stems

1 **Butcher the ducks**, placing the breasts and the legs in separate containers. Remove and reserve any excess skin and fat from the carcasses. Place the fat in a pot with ½ cup water. Place the pot over a high heat. When the fat begins to boil, reduce the heat to medium. Frequently stir the fat until the skin is crisp and it has released all of the liquid, about 1 hour. Strain the fat through a fine mesh strainer and chill.

2 **Duck Jus**: Remove any lungs or liver from the carcasses and place in a pot with the shiitake stems. Fill the pot with water to just the height of the bones. Place the pot over a high heat. When the stock comes to a boil, reduce the heat to medium and simmer the stock for 5 hours. Strain the stock through a fine mesh strainer. Place the port in a pot over a high heat and bring to a boil. Once the port has boiled, add the duck stock and reduce at a high heat until it is dark and slightly thick, about 2 hours. Strain and chill the Duck Jus. The fat will rise to the top and then congeal, making it easier to scrape off.

3 **Duck Confit**: In a bowl, combine the sugar, Kosher salt and garlic. Rub the flesh side of the duck legs in the cure and place in a perforated pan. Place the pan containing the duck legs over another pan to collect any juices and weight the duck legs. Refrigerate the duck legs for 48 hours.

4 **Preheat the oven to 225°**. With a paper towel, remove the salt and sugar from the duck legs. Be sure to remove all of the garlic as it will burn. Heat 1 tablespoon of the chilled duck fat in a wide pot. Working in batches, brown the duck legs, skin side down first. When the duck legs are browned on both sides, add the remaining fat to the pot and nestle all of the duck legs in the pot. If there is not enough fat to completely cover the legs, you'll need to flip the legs half way through cooking and add approximately 45 minutes to the cooking time. Cover the pot tightly with foil and place in the oven. Cook the legs for 3 hours. If the meat comes off with a slight tug, the legs are finished. If the meat still has a strong hold on the bone, continue to cook the legs with a tight foil cover. When the legs are finished, transfer the whole pot, uncovered to the refrigerator. These legs are best if let to sit for a few days but you may use them after 24 hours. Pick the meat off of the legs and discard any bone, skin or tendon. Store the picked meat covered completely with the duck fat. Chill the Duck Confit until needed. This will keep for a month refrigerated.

5 **Preheat the oven to 375°**. Skim any congealed fat off of the Duck Jus and bring to a boil. Keep the Jus warm. Place the pine nuts on a baking sheet. Toast the nuts in the oven until they are slightly brown and fragrant, about 5 minutes. Heat the Duck Confit in a pot over a medium heat. Place a large pan over a high heat. Place 1 tablespoon of olive oil in the pan and heat until it shimmers. Add the shiitake mushrooms with a pinch of salt. Reduce the heat to medium-high and sauté the mushrooms until they are limp. With a slotted spoon, extract about 3 cups of Duck Confit from the fat and add to the mushroom pan with the toasted pine nuts and butter. Add the spinach to the pan, cover it and turn off the heat.

6 **Place 2 large pans over medium heats**. Divide the remaining olive oil between the pans. With a sharp knife, score the fat on the duck breasts. Be very careful not to pierce the flesh. Generously salt and pepper the duck breasts. Place the duck breasts, skin side down in the pans and reduce the heat to medium-low. Cook the duck breasts until the fat has mostly rendered, about 15 minutes. Flip the duck breasts and cook on the flesh side for 3-5 minutes depending on how much you'd like your meat cooked. Transfer the Muscovy Duck Breasts to a warm area. Allow the meat to rest for 3 minutes. Reheat the spinach mixture. Slice the meat thinly. Divide the spinach mixture between 8 warmed bowls. Spread the duck breast in front and slightly on top of the spinach mixture. Drizzle the Duck Jus around and serve.

Sausage Risotto Stuffed Quail with Lingonberry Sauce & Swiss Chard

Serves 8

Quail is such a wonderful meat but I often feel it may not be filling enough on its own. We stuff the quail with some hearty risotto that both flavors the quail and gives the dish a bit more substance. The lingonberry is the Swedish cousin of the gooseberry. I have not found them fresh. They come jarred and already cooked. A cranberry sauce or apricot marmalade could be substituted here.

Sausage Risotto

6 cups chicken stock

2 tablespoons olive oil

1 small yellow onion, finely chopped

2 cups risotto, Arborio or Carnoli

2 pounds spicy pork sausage

1 tablespoon chopped rosemary

½ cup Parmigiano Reggiano, finely grated

16 semi boned quail

Swiss Chard

2 bunches red Swiss chard

1 tablespoon unsalted butter

¼ cup chicken stock

Lingonberry Sauce

½ cup lingonberries

½ cup chicken or veal stock

2 tablespoons olive oil

1 **Sausage Risotto:** Place the chicken stock in a pot over a high heat. When the stock comes to a boil, reduce the heat to medium-low. Place a wide pot over a high heat. Add 1 tablespoon of the olive oil to the pot and heat until it shimmers. Add the chopped onion and reduce the heat to medium. Add a dash of salt and stir the onions. Sweat the onions for 7 minutes or until they are translucent without any color. Rinse the risotto and add it to the pot.

Stir the risotto into the onions until the rice is shiny. Ladle approximately a quarter of the hot chicken stock into the risotto. Stir until the risotto has absorbed all of the stock. Ladle half of the remaining stock into the risotto and stir until the risotto has absorbed all of the stock. Add the remaining stock into the risotto and stir until all of the stock has been absorbed. Spread the risotto onto a baking sheet. Cover the risotto with parchment paper directly on its surface. Chill the risotto until it is cool.

2 **Place a pan over a high heat**. Add the remaining olive oil and heat until it shimmers. Reduce the heat to medium-high and crumble the sausage over the pan. Brown the sausage until it is 90% cooked about 3-4 minutes. Transfer the sausage to paper towels to drain off any excess grease. Place the sausage in a bowl with the rosemary and Parmigiano Reggiano. Mix thoroughly. Add the cooled risotto to the bowl and mix. Stuff equal amounts of the sausage risotto into each quail and set aside.

3 **Swiss Chard**: Preheat the oven to 375°. Bring 2 quarts of water to a boil with 2 tablespoons of Kosher salt. Trim any stem off of the chard leaves. Plunge the leaves into the boiling water and allow to cook for 7-8 minutes or until the leaves are tender. Transfer the chard to a bowl of ice water and cool completely. Drain any water off of the chard and place in a pot with the butter, chicken stock and a bit of Kosher salt and pepper.

4 **Lingonberry Sauce**: Place the lingonberries and stock in a pot over a high heat. When the sauce has come to a boil, take it off the heat and keep it warm. Generously salt and pepper the quail. You may want to work in batches but if you have 2 large pans, go for it. Place 2 large pans over high heats. Divide 2 tablespoons olive oil among the 2 pans. When the oil shimmers, reduce the heat to medium-high. Add the quails to the pans, breast side down. Cook the breast sides until they are brown, about 5 minutes. Flip the quails onto their backs and place in the oven for 10 minutes or until they are cooked through. Pierce the thigh muscle with a knife, if the juices are bloody, the quail needs more cooking time. Clear juices indicates you're ready to go. Heat the chard over a high heat until it is steaming. Divide the Swiss Chard between 8 warm plates. Top the Swiss Chard with a pair of Sausage Stuffed Quail and drizzle the Lingonberry Sauce around.

Seared Elk Short Loin with Asparagus, Vermont Cheddar Potato & Shallot Reduction

Serves 8

The short loin or strip loin of the elk is cut from the center ribs. It is very flavorful and tender but is prone to dryness if over cooked. This is a less expensive cut than the tenderloin. This is a dish that I will not alter or take off the menu. I've tried in the past to do such and have met with a barrage of resistance. I want to thank Prairie Harvest out of South Dakota, as their hard work has kept my elk supply steady. You may have to work in batches when searing the Elk Short Loin but the sauce is better if made in one pan.

This is an example of an emulsified pan sauce. When searing the Elk Short Loin, bits of flavorful protein stick to the bottom of the pan. By stirring the shallots, the protein bits release. These bits bind with the red wine and veal stock and produce a sauce. Swirl the pan when adding the butter as we want it to be a cohesive part of the sauce. Should your sauce break, add a touch of cold water and whisk over a medium heat. Emulsified sauces break all the time and practice is the only way to get better at resurrecting them.

Vermont Cheddar Potato

3 large Yukon Gold potatoes

1 ½ cups white Vermont cheddar cheese, chopped without any rind

4 large Russet potatoes

1 tablespoon olive oil

Asparagus

2 bunches asparagus

2 tablespoons unsalted butter

½ cup chicken stock

Seared Elk Short Loin

3 pounds Elk Short Loin or Strip Loin

2 tablespoons olive oil

Shallot Reduction

3 shallots, finely chopped

½ cup red wine

½ cup veal stock

3 tablespoons unsalted butter, cubed and chilled

1 **Vermont Cheddar Potato**: Peel the Yukon Golds and slice thinly. Place in a pot. Cover the potatoes with cold water and 1 tablespoon of salt. Bring the potatoes to a boil and simmer until they are tender, about 1 hour. Strain the water off of the potatoes and mash them or better yet, food mill them. Once the potatoes are smooth, chill them until they are cool. Combine the smooth Yukon Golds with the Vermont cheddar. You want twice as much potato as cheese. Chill the filling until ready to use.

2 **Preheat the oven to 400°.** Rinse the Russet potatoes and prick with a fork. Place on a baking sheet and roast until they are soft but still hold their shape. Depending on the size of your potatoes, about 45 minutes to an hour. Cool the Russets. When they are cool enough to handle, slice them in half so you have 8 stumps. Cut a small slice off of the rounded end as a base. With a spoon or paring knife, scoop the innards out of the Russets, leaving a nice cavity for filling. Stuff the russet shells with the yukon gold mixture. If your oven has been turned off, turn it back on to 400°. Spread 1 tablespoon olive oil on a baking sheet. Place the stuffed potatoes on the baking sheet and then into the oven. Heat the potatoes until the cheese begins to melt and the tops are browned, about 15-20 minutes. Keep the potatoes warm.

3 **Asparagus**: Bring 1 gallon of water to a boil with 2 tablespoons salt. When working with asparagus, I like to break off the ends as opposed to cutting them off. This ensures you're discarding most of the tough fibers. That said, break the tough ends off of the asparagus. Plunge the asparagus into the boiling water and allow the spears to cook for 7-8 minutes or until they are tender. Transfer the asparagus to a bowl of ice water and cool completely. Drain any water off of the asparagus and place in a pot with the butter, chicken stock and a bit of salt and pepper.

4 **Elk Short Loin**: Remove any silver skin or sinew from the elk. Cutting against the grain, slice the elk into 8 equal portions. Generously salt and pepper the elk. Place a large pan over a high heat. When the pan is hot, add the olive oil to the pan and heat until it shimmers. Reduce the heat to medium-high and add the elk to the pan. Brown the elk on all sides. Depending on the thickness and age of your meat, it should take about 10 minutes for medium-rare meat. Transfer the elk to a warm area. Drain any excess fat off of the pan, leaving approximately 1 teaspoon or enough to leave the pan shiny. Return the pan to a medium heat and add the shallots. Stir the shallots to release any bits of protein on the pan's bottom. Add the red wine and increase the heat to high. Reduce the wine by half and add the veal stock. Reduce the veal stock by half and stir in the butter. Reduce the sauce until it is viscous. Heat the Asparagus until it is steaming. Cutting against the grain, slice the elk steaks. Divide the Seared Elk Short Loin between 8 warmed plates. Top the meat with the Asparagus. Place a Vermont Cheddar Potato on each plate and drizzle the Shallot Reduction around.

Lamb Loin with Mint Pesto, Lamb Meatballs & Swiss Chard

Serves 8

I love the gamey flavor of lamb but have had trouble finding the right cut. I often find that rack of lamb can be more bone and fat than meat. Then I found the lamb loin and fell in love. This is a lean piece of meat that comes from the saddle of the lamb. It requires quite a bit of time and effort to butcher but the bones also make a lovely Lamb Jus. This preparation makes good of the extra scraps by turning them into meatballs. This is a hearty meal that does not need a starch. Should you have leftover Pesto, it's great on pasta or as a sandwich spread.

Lamb Loin and Lamb Meatballs

2 lamb saddles

½ cup chopped parsley

2 cups panko breadcrumbs

1 cup yogurt

¼ cup milk

4 egg yolks

1 cup Parmigiano Reggiano, grated

1 tablespoon olive oil

Mint Pesto

¼ cup chopped parsley

10 chopped scallions

2 garlic cloves, smashed

1 tablespoon dried rosemary

zest of 1 lemon

½ cup mint leaves

¼ cup Parmigiano Reggiano, grated

⅓ cup extra virgin olive oil

1 teaspoon black pepper

Swiss Chard

1 bunch red Swiss chard

1 tablespoon unsalted butter

¼ cup chicken stock

2 tablespoons olive oil

1 **Lamb Loin and Lamb Meatballs:** Butcher the lamb saddle. Remove the two thick loins from one side and the two thinner loins from the other. Remove any silver skin from the meat. Reserve the small loins with any fat for grinding. You may use the bones for a lovely lamb stock. Chill the thicker loins. Chop the scraps and chill them for 30 minutes. Toss the scraps with 1 tablespoon of salt and the chopped parsley. Grind the scraps through a large holed grinder and then a smaller holed grinder. When grinding the scraps, do so into a bowl set over another bowl of ice. The meat will come together much easier if cold. Chill the ground lamb.

2 **Combine the panko, yogurt and milk** and allow to stand for 15 minutes. Add the panko mixture to the ground lamb with the yolks and Parmigiano Reggiano. Mix thoroughly and form into balls the size of walnuts. Spread the olive oil on a baking sheet and place the lamb balls on the baking sheet. Refrigerate the lamb balls.

3 **Mint Pesto:** In the food processor, combine the parsley leaves, scallions, garlic cloves, dried rosemary, lemon zest, mint leaves and Parmigiano Reggiano. While the machine runs, add the extra virgin olive oil and black pepper. Set the Mint Pesto aside. This will keep for 5 days refrigerated. Wrap it with plastic directly on top of the surface to keep the Mint Pesto from turning black.

4 **Swiss Chard:** Preheat the oven to 375°. Bring 2 quarts of water to a boil with 2 tablespoons of salt. Trim any stem off of the chard leaves. Plunge the leaves into the boiling water and allow to cook for 7-8 minutes or until the leaves are tender. Transfer the chard to a bowl of ice water and cool completely. Drain any water off of the chard and place in a pot with the butter, chicken stock and a bit of salt and pepper.

5 **Place the lamb balls in the oven** and cook for 15 minutes or until they are firm. Salt and pepper the lamb loins. Place 2 large pans over high heats. When the pans are hot, place 1 tablespoon olive oil in each of the pans and heat until it shimmers. Reduce the heat to medium-high and add the lamb loins to the pans. Brown the lamb on all sides. Depending on the thickness and age of your meat, it should take about 5 minutes for medium-rare meat. Transfer the lamb to a warm area. Heat the Swiss Chard until it is steaming. Place the hot Lamb Meatballs into a large bowl and add enough Mint Pesto to generously coat the Lamb Meatballs. Toss the Lamb Meatballs in the Mint Pesto. Slice the Lamb Loins on the bias. Divide the Lamb Meatballs between 8 warmed large bowls. Top the Lamb Meatballs with the Swiss Chard and then the sliced Lamb Loin. Serve to very hungry guests.

Lamb Loin with a Pea Risotto Cake & Lemon Mint Oil

Serves 8

Peas, lemon and mint are all classic accompaniments for lamb. They accentuate the lovely gamey flavor of the lamb. This is a wonderful spring dish with bright flavors. Feel free to serve this dish with a green side salad.

Pea Risotto Cake

6 cups chicken stock

2 tablespoons olive oil

1 small yellow onion, finely chopped

2 cups risotto, Arborio or Carnoli

2 cups shelled peas, frozen are fine

8 1-inch cubes of Manchego cheese

½ cup all-purpose flour

4 eggs, beaten

1 cup panko breadcrumbs

3 cups canola oil

Lemon Mint Oil

¼ cup chopped mint

2 tablespoons chopped parsley

1 tablespoon chopped chives

¼ cup lemon juice

¾ cup extra virgin olive oil

Lamb Loin

2 tablespoons olive oil

3 pounds cleaned lamb loin

1 **Pea Risotto Cake:** Place the chicken stock in a pot over a high heat. When the stock comes to a boil, reduce the heat to medium. Place a wide pot over a high heat. Add 2 tablespoons of olive oil to the pot and heat until it shimmers. Add the chopped onion and reduce the heat to medium. Add a dash of salt and stir the onions. Sweat the onions for 7 minutes or until they are translucent without any color. Rinse the risotto and add it to the pot. Stir the risotto into the onions until the rice is shiny. Ladle approximately a quarter of the hot chicken stock into the risotto. Stir until the risotto has absorbed all of the stock. Ladle half of the remaining stock into the risotto and stir until the rice has absorbed all of the stock. Add the remaining stock into the risotto and simmer until the chicken stock is absorbed and the rice is tender. Stir in the peas and spread onto a baking sheet. Cover with parchment paper directly on the rice's surface and chill completely.

2 **Form the now cooled risotto into balls** the size of limes. Stuff a piece of Manchego into the center of each ball and form the balls into thick discs. Place the flour, beaten eggs and panko in separate pie tins or shallow bowls. Dredge the discs in the flour and then cover with the beaten egg. Dredge the discs in panko and set aside.

3 **Preheat the oven to 250°.** Heat the canola oil over a high heat. Once the oil begins to shimmer, reduce the heat to medium. Working in batches, fry the risotto cakes until they are crisp and warm in the center, about 5-7 minutes. Transfer the cakes to paper towels, to remove any excess grease. Lightly salt the cakes and keep warm in the oven.

4 **Lemon Mint Oil**: In a bowl, whisk together the mint, parsley, chives, lemon juice, and extra virgin olive oil with a dash of salt and pepper. Set the Lemon Mint Oil aside.

5 **Lamb Loin**: Salt and pepper the lamb loins. Place 2 large pans over high heats. When the pans are hot, divide the olive oil between the pans and heat until it shimmers. Reduce the heat to medium-high and add the lamb loins to the pans. Brown the lamb on all sides. Depending on the thickness and age of your meat, it should take about 5 minutes for medium-rare meat. Transfer the lamb to a warm area and allow to rest for 3-5 minutes. Slice the lamb on the bias. Divide the Pea Risotto Cakes among 8 warmed plates and top each with sliced lamb. Drizzle the Lemon Mint Oil around the plates and serve.

Veal Tenderloin with a Fricassée of Sweetbreads, Artichoke Hearts & Mushrooms with Marsala Reduction

Serves 8

Sweetbreads can be a tough sale to the unadventurous. At the beginning of each season I compose a new menu and it always has Sweetbreads on it. They sit on the menu and do not enjoy much appreciation. After only serving a few dishes and myself 2 or 3 lunches of this delicacy, I take them off the menu. Later in the season, a few guests will ask about the Sweetbreads and I have to tell them they were discontinued due to lack of demand. During the summer season of 2008, I came up with this recipe that combines two different cuts of veal, the tenderloin and the thymus gland or Sweetbread. It was an immediate hit. Those that love veal came to love Sweetbreads and those that love Sweetbreads could order the dish sans tenderloin. At last I found a way to serve a dish with Sweetbreads, a dish my guests enjoy and I get a Sweetbread lunch every now and again.

Sweetbreads

1 pound Veal Sweetbreads

2 tablespoons white wine vinegar

Artichoke Hearts

3 large artichokes

1 lemon, halved on the equator

Veal Tenderloin

2 pounds Veal Tenderloin

2 tablespoons olive oil

Fricassée

¼ cup all-purpose flour

3 tablespoons unsalted butter, cubed and chilled

1 pound oyster mushrooms, stems removed and chopped

¾ cup Marsala

1 ½ cups veal stock

2 tablespoons chopped parsley

2 tablespoons chopped chives

1 **Sweetbreads**: Soak the sweetbreads in cold water overnight. Bring 2 quarts of water to a boil with the white wine vinegar. Plunge the sweetbreads into the boiling water and allow to simmer for 10 minutes or until the outer membrane turns white. Transfer the sweetbreads to an ice bath and cool completely. Once the sweetbreads are cool, place the sweetbreads in a perforated pan. Place a container under the perforated pan to catch any juices. Weight and refrigerate the sweetbreads for 24-48 hours. Break the sweetbreads into pieces, removing any fat and as much membrane as possible. This procedure is best done with your hands as opposed to a knife that will harm the natural shape of the lobes. Refrigerate the sweetbreads until ready to use.

2 **Artichoke Hearts**: Break the stem off of the artichokes and slice off the top half with a serrated knife. I find breaking off the stem, as opposed to cutting it off, removes most of the tough fibers. Rub the cut side of the artichokes with the lemon. Place the artichokes and lemon in a pot. Fill with cold water to half the height of the artichokes. Cover the artichokes and place over a high heat. Allow the artichokes to steam for 45 minutes to an hour or until one of the leaves comes of easily. Chill the artichokes. Once they are cool enough to handle, remove all of the leaves and the fuzzy center. Slice the hearts and set aside.

3 **Veal Tenderloin**: Preheat the oven to 375°. Clean the veal tenderloins of any silver skin or fat and cut into 8 portions. Salt and pepper the loins. Place a large pan over a high heat. When the pan is hot, add the tenderloin and reduce the heat to medium-high. Brown the tenderloin on all sides, about 8-10 minutes. Transfer the tenderloin to a baking sheet and reserve the pan. Place the veal in the oven to finish cooking. Depending on the thickness of your meat, about 8-10 minutes for medium meat.
Transfer the tenderloin to a warm area.

4 **Fricassée**: Salt and pepper the sweetbreads and dredge them in the flour. While the tenderloin is in the oven, place the tenderloin pan over a medium heat. Add 1 tablespoon butter to the warm pan. When the butter stops sizzling, add the sweetbreads and increase the heat to medium-high. Brown the sweetbreads on all sides, about 5 minutes. Add the oyster mushrooms with a pinch of salt. Sauté the mushrooms until they are wilted and add the artichoke hearts and Marsala. Reduce the Marsala by half and add the veal stock. Reduce the veal stock by half and add the remaining butter, parsley and chives. Simmer the sauce until it is thick and shiny. Divide the Fricassée among 8 warmed plates. Top with the Veal Tenderloin and serve.

Petite Filet with Asparagus, Mashers & Barbeque Shrimp

Serves 8

This is my version of Surf and Turf. The shrimp are a New Orleans recipe with different variations all around the Crescent City. Although seasoning the beef is a must, don't salt the shrimp as the Worcestershire Sauce is salty enough. The size of the shrimp refers to how many are in a pound, in this case 8-12 come in a pound. Any large or jumbo shrimp will do.

Garlic Mashers

1 tablespoon olive oil

5 garlic cloves, peeled and smashed

1 quart heavy cream

5 large Yukon Gold potatoes, peeled

4 ounces unsalted butter, cubed

Asparagus

2 bunches asparagus, woody ends snapped off

2 tablespoons butter

½ cup chicken stock

Petite Filet

8 4-ounce Filet Mignons

2 tablespoons olive oil

Barbeque Shrimp

24 black tiger shrimp, 8-12 size

1 cup lemon juice

1 ½ cups worcestershire sauce

2 tablespoons coarsely ground black pepper

3 tablespoons minced garlic

6 tablespoons unsalted butter

1 **Garlic Mashers**: Place a pot over medium heat and add the olive oil or just enough oil to cover the pan's bottom. Add the garlic and reduce the heat to low. Frequently stirring, cook the garlic until fragrant. Add the cream. Simmer the cream until it tastes like garlic, about 20 minutes. Careful not to let the cream boil because it will make a huge mess. Slice the Yukon Golds and place in a pot. Cover the potatoes with cold water and add 1 tablespoon of salt. Place the pot over a high heat and when it comes to a boil, reduce to a simmer and skim off any foam. Simmer until the potatoes are tender, 45 minutes to 1 hour. Strain the potatoes and reserve a bit of the cooking liquid, to ease the milling. Do not allow your potatoes to sit in the cooking liquid. If the potatoes are left in the hot water the starch will absorb water and make the potatoes less creamy. Food mill the potatoes, adding cooking liquid as needed. Place the milled potatoes in a stainless steel pot with half of the cubed butter. Place the pot over a medium-high heat and constantly stir. Add the remaining butter and then add half the warm garlic cream. Adding as much cream as necessary, stir until the Garlic Mashers are warm and creamy. You may not need all of the garlic cream but it is great for soups or sauces. Season the Garlic Mashers with salt and keep them warm.

Asparagus

This member of the *Asparagus offinialis* comes in white, green and purple colors. The white must be grown under the soil to prevent the sun and chlorophyll from affecting the color. Choose firm, crisp stalks with compact, brightly colored heads. The darker the stem the stronger the flavor will be. When blanching, do so in plenty of water to evenly cook. Broiling asparagus concentrates the flavor. It is an excellent source of folic acid and contains vitamins A, B6, C, potassium, thiamine, riboflavin, copper, iron, phosphorus and zinc. It may contain an antioxidant with strong anticancer activity and could help fight cataracts. Asparagus acts as a diuretic and a tonic.

2 Asparagus: Light the grill. Place 2 quarts of water with 2 tablespoons salt over a high heat and bring the water to a rapid boil. Plunge the asparagus into the boiling water and allow to cook for 7-8 minutes or until the spears are tender. The cooking times will vary according to the size and age of your asparagus. Transfer the asparagus to a bowl of ice water and cool completely. Drain the ice water off of the asparagus and place the spears in a pot with the butter, chicken stock and salt and pepper, to your liking.

3 Petite Filet: Generously salt and pepper the steaks. Rub the steaks with the olive oil. Place the steaks on the hot grill and cook for about 5 minutes on all sides for medium rare meat. This temperature will vary according your grill's heat and the thickness and quality of the steaks. Transfer the steaks to a platter and keep in a warm place. Allow the steaks to rest for 5 minutes.

4 Barbeque Shrimp: Place the shrimp, lemon juice, Worcestershire Sauce, pepper and garlic in a large pan. Place the pan over a high heat and allow the sauce to boil. Once the shrimp are cooked on one side, flip the shrimp and add the butter. Incorporate the butter into the sauce through whisking and rapid simmering. When the shrimp are cooked through, transfer them to 8 warmed plates. Allow the sauce to simmer until it is thick enough to coat the shrimp. Thin with water if needed. Place a large spoonful of Garlic Mashers in the center of each plate and top with the Asparagus, Barbeque Shrimp and then with the Petite Filets. Drizzle the sauce around the plates and serve.

Herb Crusted Flat Iron Steak with Mushroom-Corn Reduction & Roasted Potatoes

Serves 8

The Flat Iron Steak is a shoulder cut that is very flavorful. It is not as tender as the Filet Mignon but it makes up for it with taste. At the restaurant, we dry our own herbs. We just lay them in a dry area for 5 days until they are brittle. If you opt to purchase the dried herbs, buy new ones as opposed to digging them out of the back of your spice cabinet. Dried herbs and spices loose their potency, after 3-4 months. If you cook the Roasted Potatoes while preparing the rest of the dish, the potatoes should be hot and ready to plate at the same time as the Flat Iron Steaks.

Roasted Potatoes

1 ½ pounds red new potatoes

3 tablespoons olive oil

Kosher salt and pepper

Herb Crust

2 tablespoons dried rosemary leaves

2 tablespoons dried thyme leaves

Mushroom-Corn Reduction

3 ears of corn, Olathe if possible

1 tablespoon olive oil

1 cup oyster mushrooms, chopped

1 cup crimini mushrooms, chopped

1 cup shiitake mushrooms, stemmed and chopped

1 cup red wine

1 ½ cups veal stock

Flat Iron Steaks

8 6-ounce flat iron steaks

3 tablespoons olive oil

2 tablespoons Dijon mustard

2 tablespoons unsalted butter

1 tablespoon chopped flat leaf parsley

1 tablespoon chopped chives

1 **Roasted Potatoes**: Preheat the oven to 375°. Place a sheet tray or sturdy baking sheet in the oven to heat. Wash the potatoes and slice them into wedges. Hold the cut potatoes in cold water while slicing the rest. Place the olive oil and 1 teaspoon each of salt and pepper in a bowl. Drain the potatoes thoroughly and add to the bowl. Toss the potatoes in the oil. Carefully transfer the potatoes to the now hot sheet tray. Roast the potatoes for 10 minutes and flip with a metal spatula. Roast the potatoes for an additional 15 minutes or until they are crispy and brown. Roasting times will vary due to different potato ages, sizes of the cuts as well as thickness of your sheet tray or baking sheet. With a metal spatula, release any potatoes stuck to the pan and set aside. You may chill the potatoes and use them later that evening, just reheat with olive oil.

2 **Herb Crust**: In a spice or coffee grinder, place the rosemary and thyme leaves. Grind the leaves until they are smooth. Set the herb crust aside. You may clean your grinder by grinding some stale bread or rice in it. The bread or rice will soak up any of the oils from the herbs and then you just need to wipe it clean.

3 **Mushroom-Corn Reduction**: Husk the corn cobs and remove any silks. Rub a paper towel or clean dish towel against the cob and most of the silks will release. If you want to get them all, use a tooth brush. Cut the kernels off the cob. Scrape the cobs with the back of your knife to release any juice, otherwise known as corn milk. Transfer the corn and corn milk to a container.

4 **Heat a large pan over a high heat**. Add the olive oil and heat until it shimmers. Add all of the mushrooms to the pan with a dash of salt. Sauté the mushrooms until they are cooked through. Add the red wine to the pan and reduce by half. Add the veal stock to the pan and reduce by half. Set the reduction aside but keep it in the pan.

5 **Flat Iron Steaks**: Heat 2 large pans over high heat. Generously salt and pepper the flat iron steaks. Divide the olive oil between the two pans and heat it until it shimmers. Add the steaks to the pans. Brown the steaks, about 5 minutes each side for medium rare meat. This time may vary according to the thickness and quality of your meat. Transfer the meat to a platter and brush with the Dijon mustard. Sprinkle the herb crust over the steaks and allow them to rest in a warm area for 5 minutes.

6 **Bring the mushroom reduction to a boil**. Add the corn, parsley, chives and butter. Simmer the sauce until the butter has combined. Slice the steaks and place them on 8 hot plates. Add the Roasted Potatoes to the plate. Top the Herb Crusted Flat Iron Steaks with the Mushroom-Corn Reduction and serve.

Flat Iron Steak with Mushrooms, Haricot Vert, Bleu d'Auvergne & Rosemary Roasted Potatoes

Serves 8

Bleu d'Auvergne is a wonderful cow's milk blue cheese from the French Alps. The name comes from the town where it is made and it is a lovely creamy and tangy delight. It gives this pan sauce depth and creaminess.

Rosemary Roasted Potatoes

1 ½ pounds red new potatoes

3 tablespoons olive oil

1 tablespoon rosemary, chopped

Kosher salt and pepper

Bleu d'Auvergne Sauce

1 pound haricot vert, trimmed

2 tablespoons olive oil

8 6-ounce Flat Iron Steaks

1 cup crimini mushrooms, sliced

1 cup shiitake mushrooms, stemmed and sliced

1 cup oyster mushrooms, sliced

2 garlic cloves, smashed and minced

1 cup red wine

1 cup veal stock

½ cup cream

¾ cup Bleu d'Auvergne, rind removed and cut into chunks

1 **Rosemary Roasted Potatoes**: Preheat the oven to 375°. Place a sheet tray or sturdy baking sheet in the oven to heat. Wash the potatoes and slice them into wedges. Hold the cut potatoes in cold water while slicing the rest. Place the olive oil with the rosemary and 1 teaspoon each of salt and pepper in a bowl. Drain the potatoes thoroughly and add to the bowl. Toss the potatoes in the oil. Carefully transfer the potatoes to the now hot sheet tray.

Roast the potatoes for 10 minutes and flip them with a metal spatula. Roast the potatoes for an additional 15 minutes or until they are crispy and brown. Roasting times will vary due to different potato ages, sizes of the cuts as well as thickness of your sheet tray or baking sheet. With a metal spatula release any potatoes stuck to the pan and set aside. You may chill the potatoes and use them later that evening, just reheat with olive oil.

Bleu d'Auvergne

Bleu d'Auvergne was discovered in the mid-1850s by a French cheesemaker named Antoine Roussel. Roussel noted that the occurrence of blue molds on his curd resulted in an agreeable taste, and conducted experiments to determine how such veining could be induced. After several failed tests, Roussel discovered that the application of rye bread mold effectively created the veining, and that pricking the curd with a needle, by providing for increased aeration, could allow the mold to enter and encourage its growth. His discovery and techniques then quickly spread throughout the region.

2 **Bleu d'Auvergne Sauce**: Place a pot with 2 quarts of cold water and 2 tablespoons salt over a high heat. We start with cold water because there are minerals that crystalize in your hot water pipes and they can discolor your food and give it an off flavor. If you prefer to add your salt when the water is already at a boil, be careful as this causes a severe bubbling reaction. When the water comes to a boil, add the haricot vert and allow it to cook for about 5 minutes or until they are bright green but with a bit of crunch. Transfer the haricot vert to an ice bath and chill until completely cool. Drain off the ice water and keep the haricot vert chilled until ready for use.

3 **Salt and pepper the flat iron steaks**. Preheat the oven to 325°. Place 2 large skillets over high heats. Add 1 tablespoon of olive oil to each skillet. When the oil shimmers, divide the steaks among the skillets. Reduce the heat to medium-high and brown the steaks on all sides. This process should take about 10 minutes for medium rare meat, depending on the thickness and age of your steaks. Place the potatoes in the oven to reheat. Transfer the steaks to a warm resting area. Place the skillets over medium heat. Divide the mushrooms and garlic between the 2 skillets. Using a wooden spoon, stir the mushrooms and release any brown bits of protein from the bottom of the pan. At this point you may opt to make the sauce in 1 skillet, be sure to scrape all of the contents of 1 skillet into the other. Increase the heat to medium-high. Add the red wine and reduce by half. Add the veal stock and reduce by half. Add the cream and reduce by a third. Add the haricot vert and the Bleu d'Auvergne. Bring the Bleu d'Auvergne Sauce to a boil and divide among 8 warmed plates. Its easiest if you use tongs to transfer the haricot vert first and then drizzle the Bleu d'Auvergne Sauce around. Slice the Flat Iron Steaks on the bias and place in the center of the plate and surround with the hot Rosemary Roasted Potatoes.

Guinness Braised Kobe Short Ribs with Cabbage and Parsnip Croquettes

Serves 8

Kobe is a type of Japanese cow that has lived the life of luxury. These lucky bovine regularly enjoy beer in the form of consumption and massage. It produces a wonderfully marbled piece of meat. The more browning your meat gets, the more flavorful the meat and sauce will be. The term braising is to begin by searing a piece of protein over a high heat and then finish the cooking process in liquid, tightly covered. If done properly, the result is moist and tender meat. The bit of chocolate in the sauce accentuates the richness of the beer. The Short Ribs will be more moist if they sit in the braising liquid overnight. You may opt to deep fry the Parsnip Croquettes. I find oven baking to be easier on the home cook.

Guinness Braised Kobe Short Ribs

6 pounds boneless Kobe or Angus short ribs

2 tablespoons olive oil

1 large yellow onion, chopped

2 leeks, white and light green parts only, washed and chopped

2 carrots, peeled and chopped

3 garlic cloves, smashed

1 cup tomatoes, peeled, seeded and diced

1 can Guinness

1 quart veal stock

½ cup dark chocolate chips

Parsnip Croquettes

1 ½ pounds parsnips, peeled and chopped

2 tablespoons olive oil

1 cup panko breadcrumbs

Cabbage

½ head green cabbage

1 tablespoon olive oil

1 **Guinness Braised Kobe Short Ribs:** Preheat the oven to 375°. Clean the short ribs by removing any fat and silver skin. Slice the short ribs into large portions and generously salt. Place a high sided pan or wide pot over a high heat. Once the pan is hot, add the olive oil and heat until it shimmers. Reduce the heat to medium-high and working in batches, add enough short ribs to cover the bottom of the pan. Brown the short ribs on all sides and transfer to a platter. Repeat with any remaining short ribs. Once all of the meat is browned, add the onions, leeks, carrots, garlic and tomatoes.

Stir the vegetables with a wooden spoon to get any browned bits of protein off of the bottom. Return the meat to the pan in one layer, if possible. Add the Guinness and bring to a boil. Add the veal stock. Once the veal stock has come to a boil, tightly cover the pan and place it in the oven. Braise the short ribs for 3-4 hours or until they are fork tender. Transfer the meat to a container. Working in batches, blend the liquid, vegetables and chocolate until smooth. Pour the now blended liquid over the short ribs and allow to sit overnight in the refrigerator.

Parsnip

Don't let the white carrot appearance fool you, these root vegetables have a fruity flesh that is reminiscent of hazelnuts. Cold weather converts the starch of the parsnip into sugar. Wash and peel before using. If the parsnips are especially large, discard the core as it is fibrous and tasteless. I find a bit of horseradish and apple accentuate the flavor of the parsnip. Choose firm, plump specimens without bruises. Avoid those that are soft, cracked, shriveled or those with dry skin. Store refrigerated in a paper towel or plastic perforated bag for up to 4 weeks. Parsnips are an excellent source of potassium and folic acid. They are said to contain six types of anticancer agents as well as vitamin C, magnesium, pantothenic acid, copper, phosphorus and vitamin B. They may act as antirheumatics and diuretics.

2 **Remove any congealed fat** from the top of the short ribs and remove the meat. Transfer the braising liquid to a pot and reduce it over medium high heat until thick. I do not like to reduce at the highest heat because bits of the sauce will stick to the pot's sides and burn, thus making the end sauce bitter. Cut the short ribs into 8 portions and reserve the scraps. If not using straight away, cover the short ribs with the sauce and refrigerate them.

3 **Parsnip Croquettes**: Preheat the oven to 375°. Toss the parsnips in the olive oil and spread onto a baking sheet. Salt the parsnips and roast until tender, about 20-30 minutes. Cool the parsnips slightly and place in a food processor. Purée the parsnips until smooth. Place the parsnips in a bowl and mix in the short rib scraps. With 2 wet spoons, form quenelles or another shape out of the parsnip mixture. Roll the shapes in the panko and set aside.

4 **Cabbage**: Preheat the oven to 375°. Remove the core from the cabbage and thinly slice the leaves. Heat a large skillet over a high heat. Once the skillet is hot, add the olive oil and heat until it shimmers. Add the cabbage and reduce the heat to medium. Stir the cabbage every couple of minutes or so, until it is thoroughly wilted. Place the Parsnip Croquettes in the oven until they are hot and crisp, about 10 minutes. Place the Guinness Braised Kobe Short Ribs and the sauce in a pot over a medium-high heat. Once the meat is hot, divide the Parsnip Croquettes between 8 warmed plates. Top the croquettes with the warm Cabbage. Top each portion of Cabbage with a Guinness Braised Kobe Short Rib portion and drizzle sauce around. Serve immediately.

Chinese Five Spice Braised Kobe Short Ribs with Sweet Potato Wontons

Serves 8

Short Ribs are such a tender treat. They require quite a bit of attention but they're worth it. Kobe beef is a luxury that I can only afford with the less expensive cut of the short rib. I cut down on the price by serving the scraps, blended with sweet potato in wonton form. This beefs up the portion and reduces waste. You may roast the sweet potatoes for the Wontons when you start the Short Ribs. The Chinese five spices are cinnamon, star anise, anise, ginger and cloves.

Chinese Five Spice Braised Kobe Short Ribs

6 pounds Kobe Short Ribs or Angus Short Ribs

5 garlic cloves, peeled

1 1-inch knob of ginger, peeled

½ cup Chinese Five Spice Powder

2 tablespoons olive oil

1 yellow onion, chopped

1 leek, white and light green parts only, washed and chopped

1 red pepper, seeds and membrane removed and chopped

1 carrot, peeled and chopped

2 cups pineapple juice

3 kaffir lime leaves

1 quart veal stock

Sweet Potato Wontons

2 pounds sweet potatoes

½ cup chevre

½ bunch cilantro, chopped

5 scallions, chopped

1 tablespoon fresh ginger, peeled and chopped

zest of 1 lime, minced

2 eggs

24 wonton or gyoza wrappers

1 quart vegetable oil

Kosher salt and pepper

1 **Five Spice Braised Kobe Short Ribs:** With a very sharp knife, remove all of the fat and silver skin from the short ribs. Cut the cleaned meat into large portions. Halve a garlic clove lengthwise. Rub all sides of the short ribs with the cut side of the garlic clove. Discard the clove and halve the knob of ginger. Rub all sides of the short ribs with the ginger. Place the Chinese Five Spice in a shallow bowl or pie tin. Dredge the short ribs in the powder and place on a grill lined sheet tray. Allow to marinate for 36-48 hours.

2 **Rinse the powder off of the short ribs** and allow them to dry to for 4 hours or pat dry with paper towels. Preheat the oven to 375°. Generously Kosher salt the short ribs. Place a wide pot over a high heat for 30 seconds. Add the olive oil and heat the oil until it shimmers. Reduce heat to medium high. Working in batches, brown the short ribs on all sides. Chop the remaining garlic. Once the meat is thoroughly browned, transfer it to a plate. To the pot, add the onion, leek, red pepper, tomatoes and remaining garlic. Stir the vegetables and scrape the pan's bottom to remove any bits of protein. Add the pineapple juice and kaffir lime leaves. Lay the short ribs in the pan in one layer on top of the vegetables. Add the veal stock and bring it to a boil. Tightly cover the pot and place it in the oven for 3-4 hours or until the meat is fork tender. Chill the meat with the liquid and vegetables, overnight if possible.

3 **Discard any congealed fat** from the top of the short ribs. Cut the short ribs into 8 4 ½ ounce portions. Reserve any scraps. Bring the liquid and vegetables to a boil. Working in batches, blend the liquid until it is smooth. Place the liquid in a pot over a medium-low heat. Add the short rib portions and keep warm.

4 **Sweet Potato Wontons**: Preheat the oven to 375°. Rinse the sweet potatoes and prick the skins with a fork. Roast for 45 minutes to an hour depending on the size of your sweet potato. When the sweet potatoes are soft, transfer them to the refrigerator. Once the sweet potatoes are chilled, remove the skins and place in a food processor with the chevre, cilantro, scallions, chopped ginger and lime zest. Purée until smooth.

5 **Chop any short rib scraps** and add to the sweet potato mixture. Beat the eggs. Brush a wonton wrapper with a bit of the beaten egg and fill with the sweet potato filling. Fill the wontons as much as possible and crimp with a fork. Repeat until you run out of filling or you have 24 wontons. Heat the vegetable oil in a pot over a high heat. Once the oil shimmers reduce the heat to medium and add a wonton. Add more wontons if they have room to fry freely. Working in batches fry the wontons for about 4 minutes or until they are crispy. Transfer the wontons to paper towels to remove any excess grease. Generously Kosher salt the wontons. If not serving right away, keep in a 250° oven.

6 **Warm 8 plates**. Bring the short ribs in the braising liquid to a simmer and heat through. Place a portion of the Five Spice Braised Kobe Short Ribs on each plate and drizzle sauce around the meat. Divide the Sweet Potato Wontons among the plates and serve. You may also include a green vegetable or side salad if you wish.

Grilled Pork Chop with Bacon Cherry Compote and Braised Cabbage

Serves 8

At the beginning of every season I try a new set up for the pork chop and every season regulars come in and ask for the old set up. This is a great pork on pork combination. If you cannot get slab bacon, use the thickest cut you can purchase. The extra bacon fat is not a necessity but makes rendering the bacon easier. This is pictured with Mashed Potatoes but whatever potato you prefer will complement nicely.

Bacon Cherry Compote

1 pound slab of apple smoked bacon, Nueski's preferred

1 cup port

3 cups pitted fresh cherries or 3 cups dried tart cherries

1 cup veal stock

Braised Cabbage

½ head green cabbage

1 tablespoon olive oil

½ cup chicken stock

Grilled Pork Chop

8 bone-in pork chops, weighing about 10 ounces each

3 tablespoons olive oil

1 **Bacon Cherry Compote**: Cut any rind off of the bacon slab and place it in a pot just big enough to hold the scraps. Add cold water to half the height of the scraps and place over a high heat. Reduce the heat to medium when the water is gone and the fat begins to render. Stir the scraps every 5 minutes, ensuring the rind does not burn and your kitchen fills with the wonderful smell of bacon. When the fat is completely rendered, strain off the scraps and reserve the fat.

2 **Slicing against the grain**, cut the remaining bacon slab into thick matchsticks. Place the bacon in a high sided pan that can hold the bacon in one layer. Add one cup cold water to the bacon and place over a high heat. When the water has evaporated, reduce the heat to medium and allow the bacon to render. Add the reserved bacon fat to the pan. With the excess fat in the pan, we're essentially deep frying the bacon in bacon fat and speeding up the cooking process. Stir the bacon about every 3 minutes to ensure even rendering. When the bacon is crisp but still tender, strain off and reserve the fat. Return the bacon to the pan and add the port. Use a heat proof spatula or wooden spoon to scrape up all the bits of protein from the bottom of the pan. Add the cherries and simmer. Transfer the Compote to a pot and add the veal stock. Simmer the Compote for 15-20 minutes or until it is thick. Keep warm until ready for use.

Cabbage

Best in the winter, these heads come in all different sizes and colors. Savoy cabbage is yellow-green and excellent in soups or as a side dish. Red cabbage has a dark purple tint and complements salads well. White cabbage has tight leaves and is good for cole slaw and sauerkraut. When buying a cabbage, choose one that is compact and heavy for its size. A cabbage should have shiny, well-colored leaves that are free of cracks and bruises. Store cabbage in a perforated plastic bag and it will keep for 2 weeks. As cabbage ages, its odor becomes more pronounced. When boiling red cabbage, a little vinegar in the water will prevent the cabbage from losing its color. Over-cooked cabbage tends to lose its color and nutrients and it acquires an unpleasant taste. Cabbage salads tend to become watery when dressed and allowed to sit. If you lightly salt and drain the cabbage before dressing, some of the water will be expelled.

Cabbage is an excellent source of vitamin C and folic acid. It is also a good source of potassium and vitamin B6. Cabbage is an excellent cleanser of the teeth and the digestive system. An anti-diarreal, antibiotic, and remineralizer, cabbage also stimulates the appetite. Cabbage combats scurvy and contains numerous anti-cancer, antioxidant compounds. The leaves of cabbage contain the most nutrients in their raw form.

3 **Braised Cabbage**: Remove any dark leaves from the outside of the cabbage. Core and thinly slice the cabbage. In a pan, heat the olive oil over a high heat. Add the cabbage and a dash of salt. Reduce the heat to medium and frequently stir the cabbage until it is fully wilted. When the cabbage has a bit of brown, add the chicken stock and reduce completely. Keep the cabbage warm until ready for use.

4 **Grilled Pork Chop**: Light the grill. Take your pork chops out of the fridge 10 minutes before grilling. Massage the olive oil into the chops and generously salt and pepper. Place the chops on the hot grill. Making decorative cross hatch grill marks, grill the chops for 10 minutes on each side or until they are cooked through. Reheat the Cabbage with a bit of the bacon fat but no salt, the fat will be salty enough. Divide the Cabbage between 8 plates and top with a Grilled Pork Chop. Top with the Bacon Cherry Compote and serve.

Desserts

221's desserts have always been simple. When we first opened in the fall of 2000, we had a pastry chef that made wonderfully elaborate creations. After a season, I discovered that to keep my labor costs down, I should start producing desserts. I was a bit shaky at first but with a firm foundation, thanks to Le Cordon Bleu, and a bit of creativity, I've developed a dessert menu that is eclectic and pleasing. I've found fresh fruit and mint take only minutes and prove to be the best garnishes.

There are a few items that I must have when making pastries and I suggest you have them at hand: heat proof spatulas, lemon juice, nonstick spray, baking sheets (or sheet trays) and parchment paper. I've designed the previous recipes to serve 8 guests. 221's desserts can not be reduced or increased to 8 portions. Hopefully you have only 11 guests that would like a Molten Chocolate Cake. Most of them depend on mold and pan sizes and cannot be altered. Use these recipes when you have a lot of people to feed. The ice cream recipes can be reduced but I love having extra ice cream around.

Molten Chocolate Cake with Chocolate Chocolate Chip Ice Cream, Chocolate Sauce & Chocolate Truffle

Serves 11

Possibly the most popular dessert at 221. There are different methods for achieving the molten center. Some insert a cube of chocolate or a frozen nugget that melts during the cooking process. I've opted to bake the cake at such a high temperature that the outside of the cake cooks completely while leaving the center gooey. It is imperative that an even coating of butter and cocoa powder line the molds for the cakes. If there are any spots not covered, the cake runs the risk of sticking and destroying your dessert. The truffles are best if they are brought to room temperature for 1 hour before serving. This allows the chocolate to soften.

Chocolate Chocolate Chip Ice Cream

4 ½ cups half and half

1 ½ cups heavy whipping cream

12 egg yolks

13 ½ ounces granulated sugar

½ cup high fat cocoa powder

1 cup dark chocolate chips

Chocolate Truffles

10 ounces heavy whipping cream

1 pound dark chocolate

½ cup high fat cocoa powder

Molten Chocolate Cakes

6 ounces unsalted butter, softened

½ cup high fat cocoa powder

4 tablespoons powdered sugar

4 tablespoons heavy whipping cream

12 ounces dark chocolate

4 extra large eggs

4 yolks

½ cup granulated sugar

1 cup all-purpose flour

¼ cup cake flour

Chocolate Sauce

12 ounces dark chocolate

6 ounces heavy whipping cream

2 tablespoons corn syrup

1 **Chocolate Chocolate Chip Ice Cream:** Place the half and half and cream into a pot. Place the pot over a high heat. While the cream is heating, place the egg yolks into the bowl of a standing mixer. Set the mixer on high and whip the eggs until they have almost doubled in volume, about 5 minutes. Reduce the speed to medium and slowly add the sugar. Increase the mixer speed to high and allow the sugar to combine. Once the sugar is combined, reduce the mixer speed to medium and add the cocoa powder. The cream should be just about to boil. Pour a quarter of the hot cream into the egg yolk mixture with the mixer running on low.

Allow the hot cream and egg yolks to combine. Transfer the yolk mixture to the pot. Place the pot over a high heat. Using a heat safe spatula, constantly stir the cream by smoothly running the spatula against the bottom of the pot. Once the custard reaches 175°, pour it into a container and chill immediately. Once cool, spin the custard in an ice cream machine according to the manufacturer's instructions. Add the chocolate chips for the last 5 minutes of the spinning process.

2 **Chocolate Truffles**: Place the cream in a pot over a high heat and the chocolate in a bowl. When the cream comes to a boil, pour it over the chocolate and whisk until smooth. Chill the mixture until completely cold and a bit hard, about 4 hours. Using a small ice cream scoop, form balls out of the mixture. Roll the balls in your hands to smooth out any edges. Place the cocoa powder in a pie tin. Roll the truffles in the cocoa powder and chill until ready to serve.

3 **Molten Chocolate Cakes**: Butter 11 custard molds with 2 ounces of the softened butter. Dust the molds with the cocoa powder. Chill the molds and allow the coating to harden, about 30 minutes. Place in a bowl the remaining butter, powdered sugar, cream and chocolate. Place the bowl over a pot of just simmering water. Stir the ingredients occasionally until they are completely melted. In the bowl of a standing mixer, place the eggs, yolks, sugar and a pinch of salt. Mix the

eggs until they are almost doubled in volume. Reduce the mixer speed to medium. With the machine running, slowly add the melted chocolate mixture to the eggs. Turn off the mixer and sift the flours over the mixer bowl. Fold the flour into the chocolate mixture until combined. Divide the batter among the custard cups and chill for 12 hours.

4 **Chocolate Sauce**: Place the chocolate in a bowl over barely simmering water. Stir the chocolate often until it melts completely. Place the cream and corn syrup in a pot over high heat. When the cream comes to a boil, whisk it into the chocolate. Transfer the sauce to a squeeze bottle. Keep the sauce in a warm area. If you would like to chill it and use it again, 1 minute in the microwave melts the Chocolate Sauce.

5 **Preheat the oven to 450°**. Place the Molten Chocolate Cakes on a large tray, leaving as much space between them as possible. Place the cakes in the oven for 13 minutes. Check the cakes to see if the tops are brown and beginning to crack. If so, take the cakes out of the oven and let them rest for 1 minute. Up end a custard cup onto a plate. The cake should come out easily. If there are snags, run a paring knife between the edge of the mold and the cake. Add a scoop of Chocolate Chocolate Chip Ice Cream, a Chocolate Truffle and decorate the plate with chocolate sauce. Plate the remaining cakes in the same fashion.

Espresso Ice Cream Cakes with White Chocolate Blueberry Crust & Blueberries

Serves 8

Originally this dessert was a way to use up any leftover blueberry muffins from brunch. It turned into one of my favorites. This recipe is good for the biceps, as it takes a good 10 minutes to whisk the eggs up to temperature. If the bowl for the sour cream and mixing cream is cold the ingredients thicken much faster.

Espresso Ice Cream Cakes

220 grams pasteurized egg yolks or 11 fresh yolks

1 cup granulated sugar

¼ cup water

2 tablespoons finely ground espresso

2 tablespoons Grand Marnier

1 teaspoon ground cinnamon

2 tablespoons orange juice

½ cup sour cream

1 ½ cups heavy whipping cream

White Chocolate Blueberry Crust

6 ounces unsalted butter, softened

⅓ cup + 1 tablespoon granulated sugar

1 extra large egg

¼ cup milk

1 cup all-purpose flour

1 teaspoon baking powder

3 cups blueberries

1 cup white chocolate chips

1 **Espresso Ice Cream Cakes:**
Place the bowl of a standing mixer in the refrigerator. Wrap wax paper around the bottom of 8 ring molds and secure the paper with rubber bands. Place a pot of water over a high heat. In a bowl, lightly whisk together the yolks, sugar, water and espresso. When the water comes to a boil, place the bowl over the water. Constantly whisk the yolks until they are thick and come to 175° on an instant read thermometer, about 10 minutes. Set the yolks aside to cool. In the bowl of a standing mixer, place the Grand Marnier, cinnamon, orange juice, sour cream and whipping cream. Whisk the ingredients on high until they are thick, about 5 minutes. Reduce the mixer speed to medium and slowly add the yolk mixture. Once the yolk mixture is combined, divide the ice cream custard between the molds. Freeze the cakes for 12 hours or until they are firm.

Blueberries

I have fond memories of gathering blueberries in Maine. It was difficult not to eat all of the berries and save some for a pie. The best preparations for fresh berries preserve their original shape. I feel that when the berries burst in your mouth you experience the height of their flavor. If a recipe calls for mashing up or puréeing the blueberries, feel free to substitute frozen berries. When buying, choose uniformly blue specimens that are free of mold. Buy blueberries that are absent of leaves and not too soft. Rinse under cold water briefly and bring to room temperature before serving.

These little treasures block the attachment of bacteria to urinary tract walls, thus preventing infection. They are high in natural aspirin and may slow loss of vision. They are also a source of vitamin C, potassium, sodium and fiber.

2 **White Chocolate Blueberry Crust**: Preheat the oven to 325°. In the bowl of the standing mixer, place 2 ounces of the butter, a pinch of salt and 1/3 cup of sugar. Using the paddle attachment, cream the butter until it is lighter in color, about 3-5 minutes. Scrape down the sides of the bowl. With the mixer on medium, add the egg. Once the egg is combined, add half of the milk. Sift together the flour and baking powder. Add half of the flour mixture to the butter mixture. Add the remaining milk to the batter and then the remaining flour. Add 1 cup of blueberries to the mixing bowl and mix until just combined. Spray a 6 cup muffin tin with nonstick spray. Divide the batter between the muffin cups. Sprinkle the remaining sugar over the muffins and bake for 10-12 minutes or until an inserted toothpick comes out clean. Cool the muffins slightly. In a food processor, place the white chocolate. Melt the remaining butter in the microwave until it is hot, about 1 minute. With the machine running, add the hot butter to the white chocolate, melting the chocolate. Break up the muffins and add them to the food processor with 1 cup of blueberries. Purée the ingredients until they are smooth. Use a spatula to spread the crust onto the ice cream cakes. Freeze the ice cream cakes for 2 hours. Serve the Espresso Ice Cream Cakes with blueberries as a garnish.

Lemon Curd with Meringue, Fresh Fruit & Candied Jalapeños

Serves 10

This is a very light dessert that is gluten free. It is a shame when those with dietary restrictions have limited dining experiences, so I try to develop menus that have choices for everyone. Make sure the bowl of the standing mixer is extremely clean. Any residual oils or dirt can prevent your egg whites from setting up. Feel free to use a smaller spoon when forming the meringue shells and serve them as bite sized desserts. Use fresh fruit that is seasonal. Exotic fruits work best as opposed to apples and pears. If your guests are wary of the heat of jalapeño, serve them on the side.

Candied Jalapeños

2 cups granulated sugar

2 cups water

3 fresh jalapeño peppers

Lemon Curd

12 ounces lemon juice, strained

12 ounces granulated sugar

8 ounces unsalted butter

16 egg yolks

Meringue Shells

100 grams egg whites

200 grams powdered sugar

1 teaspoon cornstarch

1 teaspoon red wine vinegar

1 pint blueberries

2 mangos, peeled and sliced

2 cups thinly sliced strawberries

Feel free to substitute other assorted sliced fruit: peaches, kiwi, papaya, etc.

1 **Candied Jalapeños:** In a pot, combine the sugar and water. Bring the mixture to a boil and take off of the heat. Using a mandolin or very sharp knife, thinly slice the jalapeños, crosswise. Add the jalapeños to the sugar mixture and return to a medium heat. Simmer the jalapeño slices for 30 minutes. Strain the liquid off of the jalapeños and cool them slightly. Preheat the oven to 225°. Line a large baking sheet with parchment paper.

Spread the jalapeño slices onto the baking sheet. Bake the jalapeño slices for 2 hours. Test a Candied Jalapeño by placing it on a cool surface, a chilled plate or metal counter top. If the jalapeño is stiff after 1 minute, then the jalapeños are ready. Leave the jalapeños at room temperature to cool. Carefully pick the candied jalapeños off of the parchment paper. Tightly covered, these will keep for 1 month at room temperature.

Jalapeño Chili

Choose specimens that are brightly colored, glossy and free of spots and soft patches. Without washing, store refrigerated in a paper bag and they will last for one week. Once broiled or blanched they freeze beautifully. When dealing with hot peppers or chilies, take care not to touch your face or lips. The cavity of the jalapeño is filled with seeds and white membranes. It is here that the capsacin lies, which is the spice. The more seeds and membrane you remove, the less spicy it will be. Soothe the burning sensation by eating yogurt, bread, cooked rice, sugar or sweets. Water does not reduce the heat.

Chilies kick start the blood clot dissolving system, open up the sinuses and air passages, break up mucus in the lungs and act as an expectorant and decongestant. They may help prevent bronchitis, emphysema and stomach ulcers.

2 **Lemon Curd**: Place the lemon juice, sugar and butter in a pot over high heat. Bring to a boil and reduce the heat to medium-low. Place the yolks in a bowl and whisk a bit. Whisk ¼ of the hot lemon juice mixture into the egg yolks. Scrape the yolk mixture into the pot and stir constantly. Using a heat proof spatula, constantly stir the mixture until it reaches 175°. Transfer to a container and cover with plastic wrap against the surface of the curd. The curd will develop a skin if the plastic wrap is not flush against the surface. Refrigerated, this will keep for 1 week.

3 **Meringue Shells**: Preheat the oven to 225°. Place in the clean bowl of a standing mixer the egg whites. Whip the egg whites on high until they are stiff. Sift together the powdered sugar and cornstarch. Reduce the mixer speed to medium and slowly add the sugar and cornstarch. When the sugar is combined, add the vinegar. Continue to mix until the ingredients are combined. If you mix too much you run the risk of your egg whites falling. Line a large baking tray with parchment paper. Using a large spoon, plop some meringue onto the tray. Use the same spoon to scoop out the middle, making a lovely shell. Bake the shells for 2 hours. Cool the shells completely. Tightly wrapped these will keep for 1 week at room temperature.

4 **Place a Meringue Shell on a plate**. Fill the cavity of the shell with Lemon Curd. Top the curd with fresh fruit of your choice, Candied Jalapeños and sprinkle with powdered sugar. Repeat as necessary and serve.

Carrot Cake with Cream Cheese Icing & Candied Carrots

Serves 6

The carrot cake has adorned 221's dessert menu since I bought the restaurant in the fall of 2000. It is a simple presentation but it is beautiful and quite tasty. The carrots for the Candied Carrots, need to be paper thin. Use a sharp knife if you don't have a mandolin. Making the candied carrots is a long process but worth it.

Candied Carrots

2 cups granulated sugar

2 cups water

2 carrots, peeled

Carrot Cake

3 small or 2 large carrots, peeled and core removed

¾ cup all-purpose flour

¼ cup cake flour

¾ teaspoon baking powder

½ teaspoon baking soda

1 teaspoon ground cinnamon

¼ teaspoon ground cloves

¼ teaspoon ground allspice

2 extra large eggs

½ cup granulated sugar

¼ cup brown sugar

¾ cup olive oil

Cream Cheese Icing

2 ounces unsalted butter, softened

1 cup powdered sugar

¼ cup sour cream

8 ounces cream cheese

1 **Candied Carrots**: In a pot, combine the sugar and water. Bring the mixture to a boil and take it off of the heat. Using a mandolin or very sharp knife, thinly slice the peeled carrots. Add the carrots to the sugar mixture and return to a medium heat. Simmer the carrot slices for 30 minutes. Strain the liquid off of the carrots and cool them slightly. Preheat the oven to 225°. Line a large baking sheet with parchment paper. Spread the carrot slices onto the baking sheet. Bake the carrot slices for 2 hours. Test a Candied Carrot by placing it on a cool surface, a chilled plate or metal counter top. If the carrot is stiff after 1 minute, then the carrots are ready. Leave the carrots at room temperature to cool. Carefully pick the candied carrots off of the parchment paper. Tightly covered, these will keep for 1 month at room temperature.

2 **Carrot Cake**: Preheat the oven to 350°. Grate the carrots. Sift over the carrots the flour, cake flour, baking powder, baking soda, cinnamon, cloves, allspice and a pinch of salt. Combine the carrots with the dry ingredients. In a food processor, place the eggs, sugar and brown sugar. With the machine running, slowly add the olive oil. When the oil is combined, pour the wet ingredients into the dry ingredients. Mix the 2 sets of ingredients thoroughly. Spray a rectangular mold or loaf tin with nonstick spray. Pour the cake batter into the mold and smooth out the top. Bake the cake for 30 minutes or until an inserted toothpick comes out clean. Cool the cake at room temperature for 30 minutes. Take the cake out of the mold and refrigerate it until it is completely cool, about 2 hours. If you do not plan on icing it the same day, tightly wrap the cake in plastic wrap.

3 **Cream Cheese Icing**: In the bowl of a standing mixer, place the softened butter and powder sugar. Beat the ingredients with the paddle attachment on high, until they form a smooth paste. Reduce the mixer speed to medium and add the sour cream and cream cheese to the bowl. Increase the mixer speed to high and beat the ingredients until they are smooth, about 5 minutes.

4 **Slice the cake lengthwise into 3 layers**. Line the same mold or loaf tin used to cook the cake with plastic wrap. Place the bottom layer in the mold and spread on half the icing. Top with the middle layer and the remaining icing. Place the final layer on top and wrap the cake in plastic. Chill the cake for 30 minutes to allow the icing to firm up. Cut 12 slices out of the cake and divide them between 6 chilled plates. Top the cakes with Candied Carrots and sprinkle with powdered sugar. Serve.

Nutella Crepes with Fresh Fruit & Coconut Ice Cream

Serves 8

Nutella tastes as if it is some forbidden treat. This ground hazelnut paste is full of nutrients and is perfect on a child's peanut butter sandwich. For our Sunday Brunch, we stuff it in our french toast. If your crepe batter has lumps, then it is perfect. Do not mix your batter too much as this will result in tough crepes. In the interest of making the thinnest crepes possible, you may want to adjust how much batter you add to the pan. Making crepes takes quite a bit of practice but you get to eat the mistakes. Should you have leftover batter, it will keep refrigerated for 3 days. A wide array of exotic fruit works in this dish but apples and pears seem to clash.

Coconut Ice Cream

4 ½ cups half and half

1 ½ cups heavy whipping cream

12 egg yolks

13 ½ ounces granulated sugar

1 cup shredded coconut

Crepes

4 extra large eggs

2 cups whole milk

1 cup water

2 cups all-purpose flour

4 tablespoons granulated sugar

2 teaspoons vanilla extract

½ cup unsalted butter, melted and cooled

2 cups nutella

1 pint strawberries, hulled and sliced

2 mangos, peeled and sliced

Feel free to substitute other assorted sliced fresh fruit: papaya, kiwi, peaches, cherries or melon

1 **Coconut Ice Cream:** Place the half and half and cream into a pot. Place the pot over a high heat. While the cream is heating, place the egg yolks into the bowl of a standing mixer. Set the mixer on high and whip the eggs until they have almost doubled in volume, about 5 minutes. Reduce the speed to medium and slowly add the sugar. Increase the mixer speed to high and allow the sugar to combine. Once the sugar is combined, the cream should be just about to boil. Pour a quarter of the hot cream into the egg yolk mixture with the mixer running on low. Allow the hot cream and egg yolks to combine. Transfer the yolk mixture to the pot. Place the pot over a high heat. Using a heat safe spatula, constantly stir the cream by smoothly running the spatula against the bottom of the pot. Once the custard reaches 175° pour it into a container and chill immediately. Once cool, spin the custard in an ice cream machine according to the manufacturer's instructions. Add the shredded coconut for the last 5 minutes of the spinning process.

Ice Cream

When making ice creams and custards, you must temper your yolks. This method adds a portion of hot cream to the yolks and allows the yolks to get used to the idea of being cooked. If the egg yolks were added directly to the hot cream then they would curdle, making a very rich and loose dish of scrambled eggs. Also be wary of the cream as it is heating. In a few moments, it can boil over and leave a nasty mess.

2 **Crepes**: In a bowl, whisk together the eggs, milk and water. Sift the flour and sugar into the wet ingredients. Whisk until just combined. Add the vanilla and melted butter and stir to combine. Allow the batter to rest for 1 hour at room temperature or 3 hours, refrigerated. Heat a tephlon pan over a high heat. Spray the pan with nonstick spray. Off of the heat, place a 2 ounce ladle of batter into the pan. Lift and move the pan to evenly coat it with the batter. Return the pan to the heat and allow the crepe to cook until the bottom is crisp, about 30 seconds. Flip the crepe and allow the other side to just heat through. Transfer the crepe to a tray to cool. Continue until you have 16 crepes. Once the crepes are cool, stack them on top of each other and wrap tightly in plastic wrap. These will keep for 3 days refrigerated.

3 **Preheat oven to 400°**. Spread 1 heaping tablespoon of nutella on a crepe. Top the nutella with fresh fruit. Fold the crepe in half and place on a baking tray. Repeat with the remaining crepes. Place the tray in the oven for 4 minutes to crisp the crepes slightly. Place 2 crepes onto a plate and top with a scoop of coconut ice cream. Repeat with the remaining crepes. Sprinkle with powdered sugar and cocoa powder and serve.

Almond Crusted Shortcakes with White Chocolate Mousse & Strawberry-Rhubarb Compote

Serves 6

Should you not want the trouble of making the Mousse, you could flavor a bit of whipped cream. When cherry season is ripe in Colorado, I replace some of the strawberries and rhubarb with cherries. The almonds in the shortcakes tend to make them crumbly. Add more flour if you would like more of a biscuit texture.

White Chocolate Mousse

10 ounces white chocolate, chopped

¾ ounces unsalted butter

1 egg white

1 ounce granulated sugar

3 egg yolks

½ cup heavy whipping cream

Strawberry-Rhubarb Compote

½ pound peeled rhubarb

1 pint strawberries

½ cup orange juice

⅓ cup granulated sugar

Almond Shortcakes

1 extra large egg, separated

5 tablespoons + ½ cup sugar, divided

½ cup + 3 ½ ounces sliced almonds

2 cups all-purpose flour

1 tablespoon baking powder

½ teaspoon salt

6 tablespoons unsalted butter, chilled and cut into ½-inch cubes

⅔ cup chilled buttermilk

1 teaspoon vanilla extract

1 **White Chocolate Mousse**: Place the white chocolate and butter in a bowl. Place the bowl over a pot of simmering water, make sure it is not touching the water. Stirring frequently, melt the chocolate until it is smooth. Cool the chocolate slightly. In the bowl of a standing mixer, place the egg whites. Whisk the whites on high power until they are frothy. With the machine running, add half the sugar and whisk the whites until they are stiff, about 3 minutes. Set the whites aside and place the yolks and remaining sugar into the bowl of a standing mixer. Whisk the yolks on high until they are thick and light in color, about 4-5 minutes. Reduce the machine's speed to low. Slowly add the melted white chocolate to the yolks and combine completely. Fold in the egg whites by hand until they are completely combined. Whisk the cream to stiff peaks. Add the cream to the mousse. Transfer the mousse to a container and chill for 2 hours to allow it to set up.

2 **Strawberry Rhubarb Compote**: Soak the rhubarb for 20 minutes in cold water. Cut the rhubarb into ¼-inch pieces and place it in a bowl. Hull and quarter the strawberries and add them to the rhubarb. Place the orange juice and sugar in a pot over a high heat. When the orange juice comes to a boil, add the rhubarb and strawberries and reduce the heat to medium. Simmer the compote until the rhubarb is tender, about 15 minutes.

Rhubarb

Also known as Rheum rhaponticum, Polygonaceae, the word rhubarb derives from the Latin *reubarbarum* or root of the barbarians. Initially used for medicinal properties or as an ornament, it originated in Northern Asia and is in the same family as sorrel and buckwheat. The red, pinkish or green stems end in wide veined leaves whose high oxalic acid content makes them toxic and a powerful laxative. The Europeans began to cook with it in the 18th century. It is most flavorful from February to mid March. Choose specimens that are long and thin as fat stalks tend to by pithy. The stalks should not be rubbery but firm and crisp. Inspect stalks for wilting, floppiness or browning at the edges. Rhubarb will stay fresh for only a few days, refrigerated. Stew or chop and freeze for up to 6 months.

Simmer in a small quantity of water for 20 minutes or until the fiber soften. It makes a great sorbet, marmalade, pie or cobbler. Pair tart rhubarb with creamy accompaniments to offset its tartness.

Stir only once or twice as over stirring makes the rhubarb mushy. Chill the compote until completely cool, about 2 hours. This will keep refrigerated for 3 days.

3 **Almond Shortcakes**: Preheat oven to 375°. In a small bowl, whisk together the egg white, 5 tablespoons of sugar and ½ cup of sliced almonds. Set the mixture aside. In the food processor, place the remaining sugar, almonds, flour, baking powder and salt. Process the ingredients until they are combined. Add the butter to the dry ingredients and pulse the machine until a coarse meal forms. Transfer the dry ingredients to a bowl. Using a pastry cutter, cut any large pieces of butter into the size of peas. Make a well in the center of the flour mixture. Place the egg yolk, buttermilk and vanilla extract into the center. Whisk together the wet ingredients and gradually mix in the dry ingredients. Gently fold the dough over itself a few times but do not knead the dough. Using a 2 ounce ice cream scoop, place a mound of dough on a large parchment lined baking sheet. Use the back of the scoop to flatten the dough. Leave 2 inches between each mound of dough. Spoon the almond and egg white topping onto the shortcakes and bake them for 15-20 minutes or until an inserted toothpick comes out clean. Cool the cakes at room temperature for 20 minutes.

4 **Slice an Almond Crusted Shortcake in half** and top the bottom half with a scoop of White Chocolate Mousse. Top the mousse with a 2 ounce ladle of chilled Strawberry Rhubarb Compote and the top half of the shortcake. Repeat 5 times and sprinkle the plates with powdered sugar.

Chocolate Tart with a Pistachio Crust & Port Poached Cherries

Serves 12

A simple tart with a huge chocolate punch. Serve only slivers of this tart as it is very rich. Take the tart out of the refrigerator about 1 hour before serving. This allows the chocolate to soften slightly. Substitute dried cherries for fresh as the seasons dictate. Do not use Marachino or jarred cherries as they are too sweet.

Pistachio Crust

1 ½ cups pistachios, shelled

¾ cup graham cracker crumbs

¼ cup brown sugar

¼ cup unsalted butter

Chocolate Tart

20 ounces dark chocolate chips

10 ounces heavy whipping cream

5 egg yolks

Port Poached Cherries

2 cups cherries, pitted

1 cup port

1 **Pistachio Crust**: Preheat oven to 375°. In a food processor, place the pistachios, graham cracker crumbs and brown sugar. Process until a coarse meal forms. Melt the butter in the microwave for 45 seconds or until it is completely melted and hot. With the machine running, add the butter to the pistachios and process until they are combined. Coat a tart pan with nonstick spray. Press the crust evenly up the sides and on the bottom of the pan. Bake the crust for 10 minutes or until it is golden.

2 **Chocolate Tart**: Place the cream in a pot over a high heat. Whisk the yolks in a separate bowl. When the cream comes to a boil, take it off the heat. Whisk half of the hot cream into the egg yolks. Add the yolks to the pot and place the pot over a medium-high heat. Using a heat safe spatula, stir the cream by smoothly running the spatula against the bottom of the pot. When the cream reaches 175°, take it off the heat and add the chocolate. Whisk the chocolate into the hot cream until the mixture is smooth. Pour the chocolate into the crust and allow it to cool at room temperature for 30 minutes. Refrigerate the tart until it is firm, about 2 hours. This will keep for 1 week refrigerated.

3 **Port Poached Cherries**: Place the cherries and port in a pot over a high heat. Bring the mixture to a boil and take it off the heat. Blend half of the cherries and add them back to the pot. Bring the mixture to a boil again. Keep the sauce warm. Refrigerated, this will keep for 2 weeks.

4 **With a hot knife**, slice a piece from the Pistachio Crusted Chocolate Tart. Place the slice on a plate and drizzle over the Port Poached Cherry Sauce. Repeat as needed and serve.

Bruléed Lemon Cheesecake with Fresh Fruit

Serves 12

Cheesecake is a tough game. There are thousands of recipes out there and I finally developed one that fits my pan and my oven. This is a cheesecake but with the topping of classic French Créme Brulée. Most cheesecake recipes call for a hot water bath. By heating the roasting pan in the oven, we don't have to heat the water. When beating the cream cheese, you must frequently scrape down the bowl. Pellets of unmixed cream cheese will appear in the cooked cheesecake and make it not cohesive. Use a hot knife when cutting the cake, there will be less cake stuck to the knife. Using the torch may take some practice but it is worth it. Use any fruit that strikes your fancy with this dish.

Lemon Cheesecake

32 ounces cream cheese

1 ¾ cups granulated sugar

½ cup sour cream

2 tablespoons cake flour

4 extra large eggs

¼ cup lemon juice, strained of any seeds or pulp

6 tablespoons unsalted butter, melted

1 cup graham cracker crumbs

Bruléed Crust

1 cup granulated sugar

2 cups sliced strawberries

1 Lemon Cheesecake: Preheat the oven to 325°. Place a roasting pan that will fit the spring form pan in the middle of the oven to heat. In the bowl of a standing mixer, place the cream cheese, 1 ½ cups of sugar and the sour cream. With the paddle attachment, beat the ingredients until the sugar has dissolved, about 5-7 minutes. Scrape down the sides of the bowl and add the flour. Beat the cream cheese until the flour is combined. In a separate bowl, whisk the eggs and slowly add half to the cream cheese. Scrape down the sides of the bowl and begin to beat the batter on a medium speed. Add the remaining eggs and beat until combined. Scrape down the sides of the bowl again and add the lemon juice. Beat the cream cheese until the lemon juice is combined, about 1 minute. Whisk together the remaining sugar, melted butter and graham cracker crumbs. Coat a 12-inch spring form pan generously with nonstick spray. Pat the graham cracker crust into the bottom of the pan. Pour the batter into the pan. To keep any water out, wrap foil around and up the edges of the pan. Place the pan in the center of the roasting pan. Being careful of the steam, add cold water to the roasting pan to half the height of the cheesecake. Bake the cheesecake for 1 hour. Without opening the oven door, turn off the heat and keep the cake in the oven an additional hour. Allow the cheesecake to cool at room temperature for 1 hour. Transfer the cake to the refrigerator and chill for 4 hours before serving. Refrigerated this will keep for 5 days.

2 Bruléed Crust: With a hot knife, slice a piece of cheesecake. Evenly sprinkle 2 tablespoons of sugar onto the top of the cake, it should form a thick crust. Light a kitchen blow torch and slowly cook the sugar on the top of the cheesecake. When using the torch, keep it moving or you'll have black spots. Stop once the sugar is evenly brown. Arrange the strawberries around the cheesecake. Repeat as needed and serve.

Pecan & Apple Bread Puddings with Vanilla Ice Cream & Caramel Sauce

Serves 12

Feel free to substitute different fruit as the seasons dictate. Test the caramel by drizzling a spoonful onto a plate. If it is thick, then you are ready. But if it's thin and runny, keep on simmering. I like having the puddings portioned out by my muffin tins but you can cook it in 1 pan, add about 10 minutes cook time. This recipe fills 12 2-cup deep muffin tins. If your muffin pans are a bit shallow, you'll have more bread puddings. If you did not leave your bread out to stale overnight, spread it on a baking sheet and place in a 225° oven for 15 minutes. That should make the bread nice and hard and ready to soak up some custard. These refrigerate beautifully and just need 90 seconds on high power in the microwave to heat up.

Vanilla Ice Cream

1 ½ vanilla beans

4 ½ cups half and half

1 ½ cups heavy whipping cream

12 egg yolks

13 ½ ounces granulated sugar

Caramel Sauce

¼ cup water

2 cups granulated sugar

1 teaspoon lemon juice

3 ounces unsalted butter, cubed

1 can evaporated milk

2 tablespoons corn syrup

Pecan Apple Bread Puddings

6 cups cubed bread, allowed to stale overnight

2 cups granulated sugar

5 extra large eggs

2 cups whole milk

2 teaspoons vanilla extract

1 cup packed light brown sugar

¼ cup unsalted butter, softened

1 cup chopped pecans

1 cup apples, peeled and chopped

1 **Vanilla Ice Cream:** Cut a slit down the center of the vanilla beans and place them in a pot. Add the half and half and cream into the pot. Place the pot over a high heat. While the cream is heating, place the egg yolks into the bowl of a standing mixer. Set the mixer on high and whip the eggs until they have almost doubled in volume, about 5 minutes. Reduce the speed to medium and slowly add the sugar. Increase the mixer speed to high and allow the sugar to combine. Once the sugar is combined, the cream should be just about to boil. Pour a quarter of the hot cream into the egg yolk mixture with the mixer running on low. Allow the hot cream and egg yolks to combine. Transfer the yolk mixture to the pot. Fish the vanilla pods out of the cream and scrape the tiny beans out of the pods. Return the vanilla to the pot. Place the pot over a high heat. Using a heat safe spatula, constantly stir the cream by smoothly running the spatula against the bottom of the pot. Once the custard reaches 175°, pour it into a container and chill immediately. Discard the vanilla pods. Once cool, spin the custard in an ice cream machine according to the manufacturer's instructions.

2 **Caramel Sauce**: Place the water in a pot. Pour the sugar and lemon juice into the center of the water and place the pot over a high heat. Stir the water and sugar to combine and then leave it alone. Allow the sugar to cook and when it reaches an amber color, take it off of the heat. Being careful of the steam, whisk in the butter. Add the evaporated milk and whisk to combine. Return the pot to a medium heat and allow the caramel to simmer until it is syrupy-about 30 minutes. Whisk in the corn syrup and transfer the caramel to a squeeze bottle and keep warm. This will keep for 1 week refrigerated.

3 **Pecan Apple Bread Puddings**: Preheat the oven to 350°. Coat the muffin pans with nonstick spray. Divide the bread cubes so they come up ½ way on each muffin tin. In the bowl of a standing mixer, place the sugar and eggs. Whisk on a high speed until the eggs have doubled in volume. Reduce the speed to medium and slowly add the milk and vanilla. Pour over cubed bread, to ½ way up and let sit for 10 minutes. In another bowl, crumble together the brown sugar, butter, pecans and apples. Top each muffin cup with the pecan mixture and cook for 20 minutes. Allow to cool for 10 minutes. Run a paring knife around the edges of the bread puddings and tip the bread puddings out of their molds. Place a bread pudding on a plate with a scoop of ice cream. Drizzle some caramel sauce over and repeat as necessary. These will keep for 3 days, tightly wrapped and refrigerated.

Fruit Beignets

Serves 10

Doughnuts, fritters, funnel cake are all fried dough just like the beignet. It takes a good recipe and some clean fry oil to make these into delights as opposed to soggy disappointments. We add whatever fruit is seasonal but you do not need any fruit at all. I find that blueberries just burst and are not a good idea. A good garnish is powdered sugar. A great garnish is ice cream and caramel sauce. These are great for crowds.

3 cups all-purpose flour

2 tablespoons baking powder

½ cup granulated sugar

1 cup chopped fruit, strawberries, peaches, apples, pears, mango or whatever you desire

1 cup whole milk

1 cup water

1 egg

1 quart canola oil

powdered sugar

1 **Whisk together** the flour, baking powder and sugar in a large bowl. Toss the fruit in the dry ingredients. Form a well in the center of the dry ingredients. In the center of the well, place the milk, water and egg. Whisk the egg and gradually combine the wet and dry ingredients. The batter will keep for 3 days, refrigerated.

2 **Place the oil in a pot over a high heat.** When the oil is hot, reduce the heat to medium. Working in batches add 1 tablespoon sized drops of batter into the hot oil. If the first bit of batter does not rise to the surface and have bubbles around it, your oil is not hot enough. Fry the beignets for 3 minutes on each side or until they are golden and cooked through. Remove any excess grease by transferring the beignets to paper towels. Liberally dust with powdered sugar and serve.

Molasses Brown Bread

4 loaves

Quite of few versions of this recipe have seen the inside of 221's oven. Not all were winners but after much trial and error we finally settled on the following recipe. If you do not have a large standing mixer, you can knead the bread by hand but add 10 minutes to the kneading time. This is not a sandwich bread but a great crusty bread to serve along side soups and stews.

2 cups whole milk	3 tablespoons dry active yeast	1 tablespoon salt
1 cup warm water	1 egg, slightly beaten	½ cup extra virgin olive oil
¼ cup honey	8 cups whole wheat flour, stone ground	
¾ cup molasses		

1 **In the bowl of a large standing mixer**, place the milk, water, honey and molasses. Sprinkle the yeast over the mixture. Place the bowl in a warm area and allow the yeast to proof until foamy, about 15 minutes. Add the egg to the yeast mixture. Combine the flour and salt and add it to the yeast mixture. Start mixing the dough with a dough hook. With the machine running, add the olive oil to the dough. Mix the dough until it is smooth, about 10-15 minutes. Coat 4 loaf tins with nonstick spray. Divide the dough between the loaf tins and place them in a warm area. Allow the loaves to proof until they have almost doubled in size, about 1 hour.

2 **Preheat oven to 350°.** When the oven is hot, bake the loaves for 1 hour. Cool the loaves in their tins. If not using straight away, take them out of the loaf tins and tightly wrap in plastic wrap. The loaves will keep for 1 week refrigerated and 2 days at room temperature.

Index

Chef Eliza H. S. Gavin

ELIZA'S CUISINE IS CLASSIFIED as Modern Bistro Cuisine, defined as fresh ingredients prepared simply and served in an intimate atmosphere. In actuality, it is an eclectic blend of flavors and styles. She has traveled extensively throughout Europe, the Caribbean, New Zealand, Australia and Southern United States. Eliza has enjoyed the great seafood of Seattle, Boston, Nantucket and the Chesapeake Bay. She has devoured the Southern Cuisine of Virginia, South Carolina and Tennessee. On her 21st birthday she ate a camel burger for lunch, EMU pâté for tea and kangaroo steak for dinner. She has cooked with great chefs and learned from one hundred-year-old recipes. All of these influences comprise Eliza's Cuisine. It is melange of seafood, game and poultry with accompaniments that range from Deep South to Calypso to Classical French to Californian Cuisine to Creole. It could be New American or Modern Bistro but at 221 we call it Eliza's cooking.

It all began at University of the South, at a small café in the mountains of Tennessee. Then after graduating with a B. A. in psychology in 1996, Eliza moved to New Orleans to learn about Cajun and Creole cuisine.

In New Orleans, Eliza cooked at such famous restaurants as Galatoire's and Mr. B's. There she learned about high volume establishments and how to survive on po-boys and live music.

She then left New Orleans to attend the Culinary Institute of America at Greystone in Napa Valley. Greystone is a great school for trained chefs and offers week-long classes. Eliza completed 3 of their courses and taught a class to the community representing CIA.

Eliza enjoyed Napa Valley so much that she decided to move there and work at Brix, a Pan-Asian Restaurant. After learning about Napa Valley wines and food pairings, Eliza moved to Paris to attend Le Cordon Bleu cooking school. In the winter of 1998, she successfully completed their Course de Cuisine and their Intermediate Course de Patisserie. While in Paris Eliza learned about the French wine, food and Jazz.

She returned to the United States to live in Vail, Colorado, where she learned to snowboard and wrote *Foreplay: A Book of Appeteasers*, a cookbook with 97 recipes of hors d'oeuvres. Each recipe contains at least one ingredient known to stimulate the appetite. Instead of overwhelming your guests, you prepare them for the next course.

In the fall of 1999, Eliza moved to Telluride, Colorado and fell in love with its enchanting box canyon. She began work at 221 South Oak Bistro, bought the restaurant a year later, and has been the owner and executive chef there since 2000. Her work at 221 South Oak Bistro represents the culmination of her various culinary experiences. ■